The Talking Cure

Marie-Louise von Franz, Honorary Patron

Studies in Jungian Psychology
by Jungian Analysts

Daryl Sharp, General Editor

THE TALKING CURE
Psychotherapy
Past, Present and Future

3
The Way Ahead—
Jung and Evolutionary Psychotherapy

ANTHONY STEVENS

Library and Archives Canada Cataloguing in Publication

Stevens, Anthony, 1933–
      The talking cure : psychotherapy : past, present and future /
Anthony Stevens.

(Studies in Jungian psychology by Jungian analysts ; 138)

Includes bibliographical references and index.
ISBN 978-1-894574-38-9 (v. 1).--ISBN 978-1-894574-39-6 (v. 2).—
ISBN 978-1-894574-40-2 (v. 3)

      1. Psychotherapy. I. Stevens, Anthony, 1933- II. Title. III. Series: Studies in
Jungian psychology by Jungian analysts ; 137

RC480.S84 2012 ....616.89............... C2012-904231-5

INNER CITY BOOKS

Box 1271, Station Q, Toronto, ON M4T 2P4, Canada.
Telephone (416) 927-0355 / Fax (416) 924-1814
Toll-free (Canada and U.S.): Tel. 1-888-927-0355 / Fax 1-888-924-1814
Web site: www.innercitybooks.net
E-mail: booksales@innercitybooks.net

Honorary Patron: Marie-Louise von Franz.
Publisher and General Editor: Daryl Sharp.
Associate Editor: Frith Luton.
Senior Editor: Victoria B. Cowan.
Office Manager: Scott Milligen.
Technical Support: David Sharp (www.sharpconnections.com)

INNER CITY BOOKS was founded in 1980 to promote the
understanding and practical application of the work of C. G. Jung.

Cover Image: Whorl of ancient ancestry.
Printed and bound in Canada by Thistle Printing Company Ltd.

CONTENTS

THE TALKING CURE in three volumes

Volume 3

Acknowledgements 8

Introduction 9

1 Jungian Psychology: The Personal Equation 21

2 Research 57

3 Evolutionary Psychotherapy: The New Paradigm 71

Glossary 99

Bibliography 109

Index 115

CONTENTS

THE TALKING CURE in three volumes

Volume 1 (sold separately)

Acknowledgements

Introduction

1 What Is Psychotherapy?

2 Psychoanalysis and Sigmund Freud (1856–1939)

3 Analytical Psychology and Carl Gustav Jung (1875–1961)

Glossary

Bibliography

Index

CONTENTS

THE TALKING CURE in three volumes

Volume 2 (sold separately)

Acknowledgements

Introduction

1 Ego Psychology and the Analysis of Children: Anna Freud (1895–1982) and Melanie Klein (1882–1960)

2 Object Relations Theory: Fairbairn, Winnicott, Balint and Guntrip

3 Attachment Theory: John Bowlby (1907–1990)

Glossary

Bibliography

Index

ACKOWLEDGEMENTS

This book is the result of a professional lifetime spent in the practice of psychotherapy, and, inevitably, I have sometimes drawn on material previously written and published by me. I should, consequently, like to express my thanks to the Oxford University Press for permission to use material from my *Jung*, originally published in their Past Masters Series in 1993, and to Routledge for material from *Archetype: A Natural History of the Self* published in 1982 and from *Evolutionary Psychiatry: A New Beginning*, written in collaboration with John Price, and originally published in 1996, with a greatly revised edition in 2000. In addition, I must thank Routledge and the Princeton University Press for permission to quote from *The Collected Works of C. G. Jung*, Random House for permission to quote from *Memories, Dreams, Reflections* by C. G. Jung, recorded and edited by Aniela Jaffé, and the Hogarth Press for permission to quote from *Attachment and Loss: Volume 2, Separation: Anxiety and Anger*, by John Bowlby.

I should also like to thank all those friends, colleagues and patients, who have contributed to the thoughts and opinions presented in this book. I am particularly indebted to Dr Verena Kast, Dr Wolfram Keller, Dr Tom Kirsch, Dr Guido Mattanza, Dr Frank Margison, Professor David Orlinsky, Dr John Price, the late Professor Paul Roazen, Dr Seth Isaiah Rubin, Dr Mario Schlegel, the late Dr Anthony Storr, and Dr Margot Waddell for their valuable guidance and advice, and to Professors Paul Gilbert and Spencer Millham, and Andrew Samuels, who kindly read and commented on portions of earlier drafts. I hasten to add that none of these kind people should be taken to task for any of the views expressed in the chapters that follow—except where otherwise stated, these are my own and I accept full responsibility for them.

INTRODUCTION

Well over a century has elapsed since 'Anna O.'—the patient so famously treated by Sigmund Freud's Viennese colleague Joseph Breuer—coined the term 'talking cure' for the treatment he gave her. Her case was destined to become the prototype of psychoanalytic cure, held up by Freud, and by generations of Freudian analysts, as the model of how a successful psychoanalysis should be conducted. We now know, however, that her treatment was not successful, and that the claims that Freud made for it were spurious. Anna's talking cure was no cure at all.

As a result of this and a number of other specious claims and instances of sharp practice that have come to light, Freud's reputation has been seriously compromised and the effectiveness of the whole psychoanalytic enterprise called into question. Inevitably, the contagion has spread to implicate other schools of analysis (the Jungian school being no exception) and has led to demands that the basic principles and practices of all forms of psychotherapy should be subjected to critical scrutiny and their therapeutic effectiveness (or otherwise) thoroughly assessed.

As the Freudian clinician and theoretician J. A. Arlow wrote with commendable foresight as long ago as 1982:

> We are approaching a post-apostolic era in psychoanalytic history. In a few years, we will no longer have with us colleagues who had direct or indirect contact with the founding fathers. Our confidence in our work will have to rely not on the memories of bygone heroes but on solid observational data, meticulously gathered in the analytic situation and objectively evaluated, for it is upon this set of procedures that the claim of psychoanalysis to a place among empirical sciences is based.

The 'post-apostolic era' is now well and truly upon us, and we have entered a new phase: the 'research and evidence-based revolution'. The very survival of different kinds of psychotherapy now

9

depends on their ability to provide evidence proving that they regularly succeed in their therapeutic objectives, and do so at a cost that people (as well as government bodies and trusts) can reasonably afford.

This discipline is both salutary and beneficial in that it has generated carefully conducted research programs that have established beyond doubt that psychotherapy works. From its beginnings as a treatment for the privileged few, effective forms of psychotherapy have become widely available to large numbers of people suffering from a variety of mental health problems and personal crises.

However, there has been relatively little progress in developing an evidence base for longer-term psychodynamic therapies, such as those offered by Jungians and neo-Freudians. The extensive research of recent years has failed to establish that one form of therapy is any more effective than others across a range of psychological disorders. In other words, Jungian analysis has not been shown to produce better therapeutic outcomes than cognitive behaviour therapy or psychotherapeutic counselling. This finding has come to be known as the 'Dodo bird verdict' (after the Dodo bird in *Alice in Wonderland*, who, judging the outcome of a race, gave his verdict that 'Everyone has won and all must have prizes.').

For psychodynamic practitioners of psychotherapy the Dodo bird verdict has added to the crisis caused by the decline in the authority of Freud. It has meant that they have had to take a critical look at the principles and postulates on which their practices are based. It requires a detailed assessment of how these came into being, the extent to which their present use is therapeutically valid, what research can achieve in testing and improving them, and what may be done to guide them productively into the future.

The three slim volumes of this work are offered as a contribution to this vital self-monitoring process. They are intended not only for my professional colleagues and for those entering the profession as candidates, but also for members of the public who may be contemplating therapy for themselves. Essentially, I am asking three basic questions: where have we come from, where are we now, and where do we seem to be heading?

The Talking Cure in three volumes

Each volume addresses crucial stages in the development of psychoanalytic theory and practice. Inevitably, some readers will be more interested in one stage than the others and may not wish to acquire all three volumes. Accordingly, each volume is self-contained with its own glossary, bibliography and index. For those who prefer to follow the development of all three stages, all three volumes are designed to cohere in a logical sequence.

In presenting a critical assessment of the major schools of psychodynamic psychotherapy, their history and development up to the present time, I have been inspired by Jung's insight that every psychological system (his own included) is imbued with the personal psychology of its originator. As a result, chapters in each volume that deal with the emergence of different schools begin with a biographical account, showing how their theories and practices arose as direct expressions of their creators' 'personal equation'.

Their contents are summarized below:

1: The Founding Fathers—Sigmund Freud and C. G. Jung

1. What Is Psychotherapy?
This section provides an overview of the different kinds of psychotherapy available, and summarizes their therapeutic principles. Research demonstrates that they are all effective. Since all are attempts to conceptualize the same phenomena it is not surprising that they influence one another. There are signs that they are becoming more integrated. The special case of psychoanalysis and its present uncertain status is discussed.

2. Psychoanalysis and Sigmund Freud (1856–1939)

Freud's life is examined to demonstrate his most salient qualities: his intellectual brilliance, his obsessive dedication to hard work, his outstanding gifts as a writer and extempore lecturer, his virtuoso ability to play with ideas and juggle them into new syntheses, his intolerance of criticism or dissent, his overriding ambition and his single-minded determination to succeed. Freud's most extraordinary achievements were neither clinical nor scientific but personal and promotional. With impressive tactical skill he was able to present himself as a fearless searcher after truth, totally incapable of fraud or malpractice. Now that this self-serving myth has been torn away, he stands exposed as an unscrupulous clinician, capable of bullying his patients into providing the data he needed to 'prove' his aetiological fantasies, and of generating an extensive literature that recycled a tiny number of 'classic' cases with such consummate cunning as to create the illusion of an enormous clinical database.

Yet, for all that, Freud remains an outstanding historical figure, more famous by far than any of his critics or detractors. How did he do it? The development of his theories is described and their extraordinary cultural impact analysed.

3. Analytical Psychology and Carl Gustav Jung (1875–1961)

More than any other psychologist, Jung's understanding of humanity grew directly out of his understanding of himself. From childhood he possessed a genius for introspection that enabled him to attend closely to experiences proceeding on or below the threshold of consciousness—experiences of which most people are unaware. This chapter describes how the main innovations that Jung introduced into psychotherapy arose out of the 'creative illness' (he called it his 'confrontation with the unconscious') that he suffered after the disintegration of his deeply ambivalent friendship with Freud. As Jung emerged from a near psychotic state, he recognized two personalities in himself (No. 1 and No. 2, which he later identified respectively with the ego and the Self) and proceeded to formulate his ideas concerning the collective unconscious, archetype, complex, shadow, persona, animus, anima, psychological types, and the individuation of the Self. In his therapeutic practice Jung reacted strongly against the stereotype of the classical Freudian analyst, sitting aloof and silent behind the recumbent patient on the couch, occasionally emitting *ex cathedra* pronouncements and interpretations while remaining uninvolved in the patient's anxieties and sufferings. Abandoning the use of the couch, Jung offered the radical proposal that analysis is a *dialectical procedure,* a two-way exchange between two people, who are equally involved—a model that has come to influence psychotherapists of most schools, though many seem not to realize that it originated with Jung.

This chapter examines Jung's views on the practice of analytical psychology, the interpretation of dreams, the amplification of symbols, the mobilization of unlived potential in the Self, and his therapeutic use of the biological principles of adaptation, homeostasis and epigenesis to activate the psyche's capacity to heal itself.

2: Warring Egos, Object Relations and Attachment Theory

1. Ego Psychology and the Analysis of Children

Child analysis was pioneered by Anna Freud (1895–1982) and Melanie Klein (1882–1960). They hated one another and their mutual hostility divided the British psychoanalytic movement into two, eventually three, antagonistic groups. Anna was highly gifted but never really grew up, remaining her 'father's daughter' all her life. Freud trained her as a 'lay' analyst and analysed her himself, a case of 'psychological incest' they managed to keep secret for many years. Anna, who never married, had a close relationship with Dorothy Burlingham, whose children she analysed. She published *An Introduction to the Technique of Child Analysis* in 1927 and the influential *The Ego and the Mechanisms of Defence* in 1936 as an

80th birthday present for her father. Extending Freud's topographical model (published in his *The Ego and the Id* in 1923), Anna maintained that ego defences could be adaptive as well as pathological and that their analysis required tact and a strong therapeutic alliance. The importance of Heinz Hartmann (1894–1970) is acknowledged. He sought to put Anna's work on an evolutionary basis, arguing that children are designed by natural selection to be adapted to their surroundings, thus anticipating the work of John Bowlby (1907–1990) and contemporary evolutionary psychologists. In contrast to Freud's emphasis on the father, Anna stressed the importance of the mother, arguing that child development depended less on instinctual repression than on attachment to the adults caring for them. She inaugurated the systematic observation of children and the use of research programs to test and develop psychoanalytic theories.

That dysfunctional families tend to produce dysfunctional families was certainly true of Melanie Klein's family history. To this can be attributed her lifelong preoccupation with the dominant issues of unrequited love, anger, envy, anxiety and despair. Being the victim of a domineering, manipulative mother, a neglectful father, a series of traumatic bereavements, and recurrent bouts of depression meant that she never achieved a satisfactory emotional or sexual relationship, was an inadequate mother to her three children, and provoked strongly ambivalent feelings in everyone she encountered. Alone among her siblings, she was not breast-fed by her mother which may account for the theoretical emphasis she placed on the child's relationship with its mother's breast.

To find some relief from her problems, she started reading Freud and went into analysis with Sándor Ferenzci (1873–1933) in Budapest in 1913 and later with Karl Abraham (1877–1925) in Berlin, both of whom encouraged her to specialize in the analysis of children. Impressed by her work, Ernest Jones, Director of the British Psychoanalytic Institute, invited her to England. She took London by storm, quickly polarizing opinion between those analysts who accepted her ideas about primitive infantile experiences and those who did not. The split, which was essentially about personalities, lasted the rest of the century. All Klein's revisions of psychoanalytic theory and practice (which are examined in this chapter) were systematically rejected by Anna Freud. For all their mutual loathing, both Melanie Klein and Anna Freud succeeded in making the mother and 'object relations' as central to psychoanalytic theorizing as Freud had made the father and sexual conflict.

2. Object Relations Theory

Though Melanie Klein prepared the path that led from Freudian Ego Psychology to modern object relations theories, she viewed the growing child's primary objective as striving to preserve its sanity by dealing with the psychotic terrors by which it was afflicted. It was this 'Hammer Studios' portrayal of life that the British object relations theorists were to modify. The main figures involved in these developments were Ronald Fairbairn (1889–1964), Donald Winnicott (1896–1971), Michael Balint (1896–1970), Harry Guntrip (1901–1974) and, most importantly, John Bowlby (1907–1990), who went on to develop his own Attachment Theory. Together they constituted what came to be known as the 'independent group' of psychoanalysts who, fed up with the implacable antagonism between Freudian and Kleinian factions, decided to go their own way in the spirit of 'a plague on both their houses'. Each of them developed his own theoretical orientation, and their contributions are reviewed in the present chapter. Together they introduced a more balanced, and ultimately verifiable, conception of human development. These innovations were, however, richly dependent on their own psychology (their 'personal equation') as this chapter makes clear.

3. Attachment Theory: John Bowlby (1907–1990)

Bowlby was one of the most creative and influential psychiatrists produced by any nation in the twentieth century. Not only did he revolutionize psychoanalytic theory and transform our understanding of psychopathology, but he also provided a scientific basis for the practice of psychotherapy and improved the lot of children in hospitals and institutions throughout the world. This chapter examines Bowlby's contribution in detail, particularly his preoccupation with the key issues of *attachment, separation* and *loss*—a preoccupation that was a direct outgrowth of his own life experience.

3: The Way Ahead—Jung and Evolutionary Psychotherapy

1. Jung Revisited: The Personal Equation
Since the first two volumes have stressed the importance of personal factors in shaping what psychoanalysts write, it is only fair that I should say something about my own 'personal equation'. This chapter begins by describing my own engagement with Jungian Psychology; my analysis with Irene Champernowne (1901–1976); my training in psychology, medicine and psychiatry; my research on attachment behaviour in children in a Greek orphanage (with John Bowlby as my supervisor); and my eventual emergence as a Jungian analyst. While giving strong support to Bowlby's attachment theory, I realized, in the course of my Greek research, that by overlooking the archetypal background to the mother–child bond Bowlby excluded a dimension of enormous prognostic significance, for what matters more than the personal mother's behaviour is the *archetypal experience of mothering* activated by her in the child. This realization is of enormous importance in the treatment of people with dysfunctional parental complexes, because those archetypal experiences the personal parents may fail to activate in the child persist nevertheless as *potential* in the child's unconscious psyche and seek actualization in reality. This insight represents a major advance on object relations and attachment theories in understanding the creative significance of the transference and how it can

be a determining factor in the successful therapy of patients coming into analysis, as many do, with 'parent hunger'.

This chapter also examines the contribution that Michael Fordham (1905–95) made to the establishment of Jungian psychotherapy in Britain and the United States. Founding the Society for Analytical Psychology in 1946, Fordham saw himself as an innovator who corrected deficiencies in Jung's theoretical legacy by stressing the importance of transference interpretations and analysing the influence of infantile wishes and fantasies in personality development. His advocacy of a rapprochement between Jungian theories and those of neo-Freudian, Kleinian and object relations schools, with a return to the use of the couch and of reductive analysis, led to accusations that he had betrayed the creative-symbolical approach of classical Jungian therapy, and resulted in the setting up of alternative Jungian training institutes. Consequently, Fordham's attempt to heal the split between Freud and Jung succeeded in creating further splits within the Jungian camp in England and the U.S.

I describe my attempts to transcend these divisions in my *Archetype: A Natural History of the Self* (1982) and *Archetype Revisited: An Updated Natural History of the Self* (2003), stressing the evolutionary implications of archetypal theory and the profound clinical and theoretical importance of Jung's concept of the Self, not as something created afresh by each individual in the course of personal development as the object relations theorists believed, but as an inherent propensity—a 'given' responsible for guiding the personality in its development through the stages of life. Though Jungians have so far proved reluctant to explore the rich avenue of possibilities that this approach opens up, it is nevertheless being adopted by the new breed of evolutionary psychotherapists. I argue that their work needs to be done in the spirit of Jung's broad humanity and open-mindedness, and his understanding of the healing potentials inherent in the Self.

2. Research

Research showing that elaborate long-term analysis is not indispensable to favourable outcome threatens the very survival of traditional forms of analytic therapy. This chapter presents the evidence and gives critical examination to the Dodo bird verdict, arguing that the use of 'meta-analysis' to homogenise the results of thousands of different studies with hundreds of different client groups is inevitably going to obscure important differences between them. Meta-analysis served its purpose in demonstrating that all forms of psychotherapy work, but what researchers are increasingly having to examine is the issue of what works best for whom. The crucial questions for research to address were asked as long ago as 1967 by Gordon Paul: '*What* treatment, by *whom*', he wrote, 'is most effective for *this* individual with *that* specific problem, and under *which* set of circumstances?' Researchers are refining their techniques and some of Paul's questions are being answered, but there is still much ground to be covered. Features contributing to favourable outcome common to all therapies are increasingly understood and are carefully summarized. What research has great difficulty in assessing is the quality of the exchanges that occur in an analytic session: here the line between science and art grows hazy.

3. Evolutionary Psychotherapy

The views of different schools on the causes and treatment of psychological disorders are summarized and compared with the views current among evolutionary psychiatrists and psychotherapists. This chapter presents a crash course in evolutionary psychiatry, revealing its close compatibility with Jungian theory. Evolutionary psychiatry maintains that evolution has equipped us with a large repertoire of genetically encoded psychological mechanisms (Jung's archetypes of the collective unconscious) which enable us to respond adaptively to social and physical environmental events. Symptoms are not seen as signs of 'disease' but natural responses that can become distorted or exaggerated in response to contemporary environmental pressures, or as the result of 'the frustration of archetypal intent'.

Symptoms are thus richly meaningful adaptations. The evolutionary history and the selective advantages of anxiety, phobia, mania and depression are described and their psychopathology and treatment in contemporary patients, explained. In Jungian terms, these disorders provide examples of an archetype entering the personal psyche as a complex. To suffer from a phobia is to experience what it is to be in the grip of an 'autonomous complex'. A new classification of the major psychiatric disorders emerges. The 'biosocial goals' listed by evolutionary psychologists correspond neatly to the foci of interest of the main schools of analysis. The objections to applying Darwinian insights to human psychology are sympathetically examined, and shown to be mistaken.

Whatever upheavals may be in store for us as a result of theoretical revisions, outcome studies, clinical audits, and research on the biochemistry of the brain, the primary duty of the psychotherapist will remain the same: to put empathy, knowledge and professional skill at the service of the patient. To adopt an evolutionary approach is not to espouse a political cause, to submit to biological determinism or to abandon a proper concern for ethical values. What such an approach does provide is a compass and a new orientation to steer us through the immense complexities of human psychology, its disorders and their treatment.

1

JUNGIAN PSYCHOLOGY: THE PERSONAL EQUATION

In the first two volumes of this book I have stressed the importance of personal factors in shaping what psychoanalysts write. So it is only fair that I should say something about my own 'personal equation'. The most crucial decisions in peoples' lives are often taken in a remarkably haphazard manner. My own decision to become an analyst was no exception.

It was made late one evening when I was 16 years old. I was alone and already in bed when I turned on my radio tuned to the BBC Third Programme. A play was just beginning. To the sound of waves crashing against rocks, a narrator announced that we were at Elsinore and that the recently crowned King Claudius is worried by the odd behaviour of his nephew, Hamlet. Accordingly Claudius has sent to Paris for a celebrated doctor, a specialist in distempers of the mind, and invited him to Denmark so that he may study the Prince and discover what ails him.

Shakespeare's play begins, and at critical moments the doctor is heard making *sotto voce* interpretations of Hamlet's state of mind. Like some psychological Sherlock Holmes, he picks up clues which enable him to diagnose the essence of Hamlet's problem: Hamlet is incestuously tied to his mother, Gertrude, and cannot obey the command he has received from his father's ghost to kill his uncle Claudius, because *Claudius has done precisely what Hamlet himself unconsciously wished to do*—namely murder the old king (Hamlet's father) and take possession of Gertrude (his mother). Locked in this unconscious predicament, Hamlet's will is paralysed, which explains his incorrigible procrastination. This play greatly excited me: it seemed to give me a clear image of what to do with my life. As the play ended, I knew with absolute certainty that *I must become that doctor.*

Of course, I later came to realize that the play (incidentally,

21

based on a paper by Freud's biographer Ernest Jones) moved me so deeply because it touched on my own family situation—an only child with an adorable mother and a kind but very introverted father, who was frequently away on business, leaving me to fill the emotional vacuum in my mother's life. The sort of understanding possessed by the doctor offered a way out of my own predicament: how to escape entanglement in my parents' marriage and establish a life of my own, with, one hoped, less tragic consequences than befell Hamlet and his entire family.

So much became clear when I entered analysis at the age of 23. I was particularly fortunate in my analyst, Irene Champernowne (1901–1976). Even allowing for an inevitable degree of idealization on my part, she was one of the shrewdest and most impressive women I have ever met. She was widely experienced and well read in the major analytic traditions of her time. Having had a Freudian analysis at the Tavistock Clinic in the late 1920s, she spent half of each year during the early 1930s working with Alfred Adler in Vienna and later analysing with Adler's colleague Leonard Seif in Munich, before moving on to Zurich to analyse with Jung and Toni Wolff. Though she came from an intensely religious family (her father was a missionary), she had elected to read for a science degree at Birkbeck College and went on to become a lecturer in biology at Gypsy Hill Teachers' Training College in London. She was an inspired teacher and found that students in personal difficulties gravitated to her as an untrained but natural counsellor.

The course of her life changed in her mid-twenties when she suffered a religious crisis, became seriously depressed, and got herself into analysis. When she eventually reached Zurich she had a profound sense of spiritual homecoming, for Jung's approach drew together the three primary interests of her life: psychology, religion and biological science. It struck her that Jung had reconciled the highest achievements of the human spirit with the base materials out of which that spirit had evolved. She said that it was as if Jung had succeeded in building a bridge between Darwin and God! The theory of archetypes provided 'the missing link between psyche and nature'.

As she told me on one memorable occasion, archetypes could be conceived as biological entities which had evolved by natural selection: they achieved their highest expression in the production of culture and the organization of human consciousness. This hit me with the force of a revelation. It was a tremendous statement, and it seemed to me that in making it Irene had struck the bedrock of psychology as a biological science. It is an insight that has much influenced my thinking ever since.

When my analysis began I was in my preliminary year as a medical student at Oxford. Before going to Oxford I had spent three years at Reading University where I obtained a BA honours degree in Psychology. At that time, Psychology Departments were still in the grip of Behaviourism, and students were required to study the huge literature on learning experiments performed on rats running in mazes. This was as dispiriting for the students as it must have been for the rats.

Fortunately, the Professor of Psychology at Reading, Carolus Oldfield, though a behaviourist, had sufficient vision to look ahead to a time when psychology should be established as a science compatible with Darwinism. To this end he had in his department a physiologist with a particular interest in animal behaviour called, appropriately enough, Dr Voles, and it was from Dr Voles that I first learned about ethology and the work of Niko Tinbergen and Konrad Lorenz. As a result, the experimental work I did as the basis for my degree thesis was not on rats, or for that matter on human beings, but on 'Colour and Brightness Discrimination in the Three-Spined Stickleback'. This, I will be the first to admit, was no great contribution to the sum total of human knowledge, but it taught me the rudiments of scientific method and experimental design, which was to come in handy later on.

At Reading I had the luck to be the only Psychology student in my year. This meant that I was able to enjoy a closer relationship with my lecturers than would otherwise have been the case. My tutor in Psychopathology was a colourful character called David Stafford-Clark, author of the bestselling Penguin *Psychiatry Today*, who later became a television celebrity. He was a consultant at Guy's Hospital, and arranged for me to spend a day each week with him, seeing patients and attending case conferences. This experience confirmed in me a conviction that I must become a psychiatrist, as well as an analyst and a psychologist.

A curious fact of life at Oxford was that medicine was not considered a subject worthy of an honours degree and one was required to spend an added year doing Anatomy or Physiology, which, for some reason known only to the university authorities, were acknowledged as honours subjects. It was also possible to do an honours degree in Psychology, Philosophy and Physiology (known as 'PPP'), but that took two years. By a happy coincidence, Carolus Oldfield was appointed to the chair of Psychology at Oxford soon after I had enrolled there as a medical student, and as I already had one degree in psychology Carolus arranged for me to do the PPP course in one year instead of two. This, as it turned out, was not a waste of time, for it enabled me to extend my knowledge of Ethology and Physiology, and to learn more about the intricacies of planning research.

My analysis with Irene continued with brief interruptions for nearly five years and was the most important period of my life. It ignited creative sparks in me which, touch wood, have so far shown few signs of being dimmed. Her greatest gift was the ability to bring to life unlived potential that I had no idea I possessed. To her, the collective unconscious was not just a scientific theory but an empirical fact—a vital, continuously present 'companion of the way'. Though having good friends of my own age, I had, before my analysis, felt isolated in my personal cocoon, painfully different from everyone else. But Irene's understanding of the archetypal symbolism emerging in my dreams and paintings drew me into a recognition of my identity as a fully paid-up member of the human

24

race. That, combined with the overflowing warmth of her personality, was profoundly healing, and it stood me in good stead for the rest of my life. There can be no doubt that for me Jungian analysis worked. Whether this was because of Irene's ability as a therapist or because of the effectiveness of Analytical Psychology itself I was not at the time sure—but, that my horizons widened, that my capacity to understand myself and others grew, that my ability to share love deepened, that I felt personally enriched, was as evident to me as it was to my nearest and dearest.

By the time I was medically qualified, my analysis was over and I had fallen in love with Greece. This began on the island of Samos, where I was the guest of an Oxford friend who had rented a cottage for three months. The blight of mass tourism still lay in the future and we were virtually the only foreigners on that idyllic island. We were treated with immense kindness by the locals and, my mind being hyperactive after medical finals, I rapidly learned pretty basic Modern Greek.

On my way back to England to start my first intern 'house job' I lingered in Athens, where I was introduced to Spyros Doxiadis, a Professor of Paediatrics and medical director of a progressive orphanage for unwanted children called the Metera Babies Centre. Impressed by my background in Psychology, he offered me a research fellowship in infant behaviour at the Metera to be taken up when my pre-registration house jobs were completed.

I have described my time at the Metera in *Archetype: A Natural History of the Self* (1982) and so I will repeat here only what is germane to my development as an analyst. What was remarkable about the Metera was that Spyros Doxiadis and his staff had taken Bowlby's findings very much to heart, with the result that their policy was to provide every child, for as long as the Metera was its home, with a substitute mother with whom it might share that warm, intimate, continuous relationship which Bowlby regarded as indispensable to normal human development. When I took up my research appointment there in the spring of 1966, 96 nurses were employed to look after as many infants. The soulless anonymity of traditional institutions was avoided by splitting up the community of nurses and children into small, relatively autonomous groups, each centred on one of eight separate pavilions. Each pavilion contained twelve children, and, in accordance with the 'family grouping' or 'key worker' system devised by Anna Freud and Dorothy Burlingham, their cots were arranged in four compartments with three nurses allocated to each. As a result, both medical and senior nursing staff appeared satisfied that every child was receiving intensive care from a small number of women—much as a normal family-reared Greek child might be looked after by its mother, grandmother and eldest sister.

It seemed an admirable arrangement. But within days of beginning my research, it became clear to me that the only occasion on which this system worked satisfactorily was when the matron made her rounds. As soon as she departed, the nurses and the youngest children interacted to an extraordinary degree, so that in the course of a few hours each nurse came into contact with practically every child in the pavilion. A form of maternal communism reigned in which caretaking was shared—from each according to her ability, to each according to his need.

This was an exciting discovery. For I realized that I had fallen into a situation that was perfectly set up to test the two rival theories of infant attachment formation, which were then the subject of unresolved controversy. On the one hand was the theory, supported by Anna Freud as well as the behaviourists, that infant attachment was learned through a form of operant conditioning associated with natural rewards and punishments, and on the other hand was Bowlby's theory that it was instinctive.

As Anna Freud (1946) put it: 'When its powers of perception permit the child to form a conception of the person through whose agency it is fed, its love is transferred to the provider of the food'. This theory, known as the 'cupboard love theory' still had the greater number of adherents, though Bowlby's 'ethological' theory was gaining ground. The Metera offered a perfect milieu in which to test the relative validity of these two theoretical positions.

My reasoning ran like this: if the cupboard love theory were valid, it must follow that children receiving care from such a large number of mother-figures would become attached to all the nurses who regularly cared for them. Moreover, the nurses to whom a child became attached would necessarily be arranged in a hierarchy of preference, the nurses at the top of the hierarchy being those who fed him the most.

If, on the other hand, Bowlby's theory were valid, the outcome would be very different. In the environment in which our species evolved (the 'environment of evolutionary adaptedness' or the 'ancestral environment'), the women responsible for an infant's care would be few in number (usually the mother and perhaps a close relative), and the innate mechanism controlling the development of attachment would tend to focus only on one or two figures.

The tendency for an innately determined behavioural system to take as its goal a particular individual or a small group of individuals Bowlby believed to be a biological characteristic of our species, and he gave it a name: he called it *monotropy*. If Bowlby were right, therefore, a Metera child would not become attached to the majority of its caretakers as the cupboard love theory would predict, but would come to demonstrate clear preference for one nurse above all the rest.

It was almost too good to be true. All I had to do was select a group of infants and make regular observations of their social progress. Quickly I chose 24 unattached children aged three months and above, and, with two assistants, began recording their interactions with their nurses. Within six months I had collected enough data to establish beyond doubt that far from becoming attached to all their nurses, 75 per cent of the children became specifically attached to one nurse, who was preferred way above all the rest. Even by the strictest statistical criteria, allowing for the small size of the sample, Bowlby's monotropic principle was confirmed. The 25 per cent who did not display attachment had left the Metera for adoption before the age at which specific attachment becomes apparent.

What effectively 'did for' the cupboard love theory was my finding that no less than one-third of the children became attached to nurses who had done little or nothing in the way of routine caretaking of the child before the attachment bond had been formed. The crucial factors leading up to the paring off of a particular nurse with a particular child were not so much linked with routine feeding as with play, physical contact and social interaction; the whole process was more akin to falling in love through mutual delight and attraction than to 'operant conditioning'.

Having established this much in direct observational terms, I began a detailed study of the typescripts of tape-recorded interviews I had personally conducted with each of the nurses to whom the children in my sample had become attached. As I did so, I began to feel uneasy. Although Bowlby was undoubtedly right, it seemed to me that his theory did not pay adequate attention to certain aspects of the attachment phenomenon that I came to see as possessing great significance.

In the course of these interviews I had asked each nurse what she thought it was that had motivated her and her infant to become attached to one another. Without exception, they all replied that it was 'love'. My attempts to probe what they understood by this elusive concept indicated that they used 'love' to describe the subjective emotion of fondness, solicitude and delight which accompanied caresses, kisses, tender words, eye-to-eye contacts, smiles, songs and tickling games. They spoke freely of their child's personal attractiveness, popularity, charm, and evident need for themselves. Although their statements often betrayed their lack of psychological sophistication, much of what the Metera nurses said had a fresh, original quality that possessed the virtue of being uninfluenced by psychoanalytic dogma and second-hand beliefs. Their observations provided me with a timely reminder that *attachment* is the synonym of *love*.

Mother and father: archetypes and complexes

These thoughts compelled me to acknowledge that there are serious limitations to the application of the ethological approach to human psychology. The Metera nurses had taught me, in their innocence, that if we are not very careful, we could allow ethology to lead us into the same reductive trap as had imprisoned the behaviourists, the Freudians and the Kleinians. Preoccupation with the detailed investigation of behavioural systems, fascinating though such studies can be, might well yield not a unified science of humanity so much as an arid technology which seeks to boil down the infinitely rich phenomena of life to the last 'innate psychological mechanism'. In particular, the difference in emphasis between the Metera nurses' reports and the observational data presented me with a problem.

How was one to bring all aspects of the attachment phenomenon within the ambit of a single theoretical formulation that honoured the subtle complexities involved? What I needed was a comprehensive theory capable of embracing both the behavioural manifesttations of attachment and the inner psychic experiences occurring in consciousness in the form of symbols, images, feelings and words. The more I thought about it, the more clear it became to me that the theory I was attempting to formulate already existed in the form of Jung's theory of archetypes.

Jung's original insights into the archetypal processes underlying the mother–child relationship were developed by his Israeli colleague Erich Neumann in two books, *The Great Mother: An Analysis of the Archetype* (1955) and *The Child: Structure and Dynamics of the Nascent Personality* (1973). Both these works suffer from the disadvantage that Neumann's biology was even shakier than Jung's and much more subject to Haeckelian and Lamarckian influences. However, when shorn of these unfortunate accretions, the Jungian position is impressive. It must be remembered that when Jungians speak of a mother archetype they are not referring to an innate image but to an inner dynamic at work in the phylogenetic

29

psyche. Symbolic expressions of this dynamic are found in the myths and artistic creations of humanity. As Mother Nature and Earth Mother, the archetypal mother is celebrated as goddess of fertility and dispenser of nourishment; as water or sea, she represents the origins of life as well as a symbol of the unconscious, the fount of all psychic creativity; as Moon Goddess, she exemplifies the essential periodicity of womanhood. She also takes the form of divine animals: the bear (jealous guardian of her children); the celestial cow, who nourishes the earth with milky rain.

Like all archetypes, the Great Mother possesses both positive and negative attributes. On the one hand, she is creative and loving; on the other, she is destructive and hateful. This paradox on the mythological plane corresponds to the observation shared by all schools of analysis that children are deeply ambivalent in their feelings and behaviour towards their mothers. Where the schools differ is in their explanation of how the 'good' and 'bad' images of the mother are formed. As we have seen, the object relations school sees these as 'introjected' internal objects based on the child's actual experiences of the personal mother. Jungians, however, see them as symbolic actualizations of the Good Great Mother and the Terrible Mother archetypes respectively. In other words, the child is phylogenetically 'forewarned' of the mother's inevitably dual nature: she who caresses also slaps, she who gives also withholds, she who grants life may also take it away.

Whereas the Good Mother's symbols are the flowing breast, the abundant cornucopia, the fruitful womb—the Terrible Mother is the bloodstained goddess of death and destruction: she is Kali dancing on the hapless form of Shiva; she is Rangda with slobbering mouth and great lolling tongue who steals and devours children; she is the Gorgon with writhing snakes hissing about her head, so hideous that she turns men to stone when they look at her. The animal forms that she most characteristically adopts are the dragon and the devouring sea serpent with whom the heroes of countless mythologies have grappled down the aeons of time.

Both 'Good' and 'Terrible' aspects of the mother archetype influence the behaviour of mother and child at a predominantly unconscious level of psychic activity. Activation of either aspect results in what Neumann calls 'a state of biopsychical seizure', a compelling state of possession that drives the behaviour of the subject and is associated with powerful emotional accompaniments. When the Good Mother rules, all is peace and contentment; but should the Terrible Mother be activated, pandemonium is the result: inconsolable screaming in the child (often rationalized as 'teething', 'colic' or 'wind'), fury, even battering by the mother (who, in retrospect, may find her own behaviour incredible and deeply shaming when the 'biopsychical seizure' has passed).

Clearly, it is important for the stability of the attachment bond and the health of the child that the mother should succeed overall in constellating the Good, rather than the Terrible Mother. When one appreciates the symbolic power of the archetypes involved, the truth of this statement becomes very apparent, yet, in his neglect of the archetypal psychic background to the attachment bond, Bowlby excluded a dimension of enormous prognostic significance. What matters from the point of view of healthy psychic development is not always the actual behaviour and personality of the mother as Bowlby supposed, but the *archetypal experiences actualized by her* in the child.

The critical factor for psychopathology, in the Jungian view, is not so much the actual mother but the mother complex which is formed within the individual's psyche. This complex is no inner 'video-recording' of the personal mother-out-there, but a product of her interaction with specific evolved components in the child's maturing psyche.

This fact, with all its implications, has to be grasped if success is to be achieved in the psychotherapy of people with dysfunctional parental complexes. For those archetypal components that the personal parents succeed in actualizing in their child may not be as crucial for his individual destiny as those that they fail to actualize.

31

As children, we all begin by experiencing our parents as infallible, vividly numinous embodiments of the Mother and Father archetypes; only later, as we attain years of discretion, do we recognize them as fallible human beings with their own personal limitations.

Theoretically, every archetype possesses a totality; individual parents, however, being human and not gods, are by their very nature imperfect and incomplete—consequently, they can never hope to embody in their own lives all the attributes of a parental archetype. All that any parent can realistically aim to be is 'good enough', to use Winnicott's phrase, to provide the key that opens the archetypal lock and, in doing so, realize that the parental archetype so released will profoundly influence the child's expectations. As we ourselves discover when we grow up, children always expect more of us than we have to give them and, when we disappoint them, they go off to seek what they want elsewhere. It would be cruel and ungrateful were it not that each generation repays what it owes to the last by giving to the next.

Repeatedly it is found in practice that whatever archetypal characteristics parents may have failed to activate nevertheless persist as *potential* in the child's unconscious psyche and they continue to seek actualization in reality. Indeed, it is this need to actualize unlived potential that brings patients to therapy in the first place. The extent of this unactualized potential is inversely proportional to the parents' effectiveness: the more incompetent they are, the greater the archetypal potential seeking fulfilment and the greater the 'parental hunger' manifested by the child (hence, for example, the 'clinging' children one encounters in institutions).

A major theoretical advance

This Jungian concept of innate archetypal potential available to be activated to a greater or lesser extent by appropriate figures in the environment is a major theoretical advance beyond object relations and attachment theories. Not only does it provide a unitary explanation of both outer behaviour and inner experience, but it also counts for some of the most impressive findings in clinical practice.

I was later to publish reports of a number of cases to illustrate this point, but the person who sticks most vividly in my memory is a woman who came to me with a father complex that had blighted much of her life. Her personal father had been a tyrant, who insisted always on having his own way and made terrifying scenes whenever he was thwarted. As a result, the father archetype had been activated in her psyche, but only in the most partial and destructive manner: only the law-giving, authoritarian aspects of the father archetype were built into her father complex, while the loving, protective aspects of the archetype remained in the unconscious as unactivated potential.

The result was that throughout her life this woman seemed fated to be drawn into the orbit of bullying, self-righteous men, whom she felt she had no alternative but to placate, appease and obey. At the same time, there persisted in her an unfulfilled longing for the man who would do none of these things to her but, on the contrary, would give her love, support and protection.

Unfortunately, she could never seem to find him, for she could never get into a relationship with such a man: he was too alien, too essentially unfamiliar to her, and she did not possess the emotional vocabulary necessary to share such love.

In the initial stages of her analysis, her father complex inevitably got into the transference: unconsciously she would project the 'imago' of the tyrannical father on to me, as became clear when she misinterpreted my words or gestures as signs that I was becoming furious with her for not being a better patient!

At other times, her dreams, fantasies and behaviour revealed how much she longed for me to bring into living reality the positive father potential that remained unactualized in her unconscious. This, I realized, was another aspect of the transference that none of the object relations analysts had detected because their thinking lacked the archetypal dimension. *There was in the transference not only the father she had, but also the father she never had but longed for.*

As the analysis progressed, she was able to become conscious of the destructive influence of her father complex, to find the strength to stand up to the men who bullied and exploited her, and to distance herself from them, integrating some of their authority in her own personality. Gradually, a warm, trusting relationship, freed of negative projections, developed between us. This resulted in activation of enough positive father potential for a healthier and more supportive father complex to form in her psyche. As a consequence, the capacity to relate to decent men, who were kindly disposed to her, began to improve.

This analysis, which was one of the first I conducted under Irene's guidance, brought home to me the fact that the more unconscious a complex, the more readily it is projected onto figures in the environment who correspond in certain ways to essential characteristics of the complex. So it was that my patient projected her complex on to men possessing qualities reminiscent of her father and then proceeded to become, much against her will, the victim of their sadistic power. The advantage of Jung's insight into the nature of archetypes and their mode of actualization in the form of complexes provided me with both an understanding of my patient's condition and the means to help her grow beyond it. The result was that her individuation, which had hitherto been blocked, was now freed to proceed on its way.

The question of training

My training as an analyst was something of an anachronism. It resembled that of all analysts, both Freudian and Jungian, before official training institutes came into existence. In those days one had a personal analysis with Freud or Jung, or one of their associates, attended their meetings or seminars when they conducted them, read intensively, and then started to see patients.

The idea of performing 'control' analyses under supervision was a comparatively late innovation. For example, when Max Eitingen, a Swiss psychiatrist from the Burghölzli, came to Vienna in 1907, Freud analysed him as they strolled through the streets and parks.

Neither Freud nor Jung had any formal analysis, except on their journey to and from the United States in 1909, when they analysed each other's dreams—an activity which ended in stalemate, since Freud censured his associations rather than compromise his authority. (When he did that, commented Jung, he lost it anyway!)

Freud's translator James Strachey, describing how he became a psychoanalyst in the early 1920s, recalled that he had 'no medical qualifications, no knowledge of the physical sciences, no experience of anything except third-rate journalism. The only thing in my favour,' he said, 'was that at the age of thirty I wrote a letter out of the blue to Freud, asking if he would take me on as a student. For some reason, he replied, almost by return of post, that he would, and I spent a couple of years in Vienna.'

When Strachey returned to London he was at once elected an associate member of the British Psycho-Analytical Society. 'So there I was,' he said, 'launched on the treatment of patients, with no experience, with no supervision, with nothing to help me but some two years of analysis with Freud.' As we have seen, the training received by Anna Freud, Melanie Klein, Ronald Fairbairn, Donald Winnicott (who was himself analysed by James Strachey) and Harry Guntrip was very similar.

Irene Champernowne's training had been somewhat more systematic. After her initial analyses with Jung and Toni Wolff in Zurich, she returned to London and continued to analyse with Jung's chief lieutenant in England, Dr Godwin Baynes. They got on so well that in 1938, her analysis concluded, Baynes invited her to share in his analytic practice, giving her the use of a consulting room in his house in Mansfield Street. This arrangement continued until they were driven out of London by the Blitz in 1941. It was through working as Baynes's colleague that Irene learned her craft, rather in the manner of a medieval apprentice. They popped in and out of each other's rooms for impromptu case conferences between patients' appointments and regularly had working lunches at the Bolivar Restaurant round the corner. Irene always believed this was the best way for analysts to learn their job, and it was the way that I, eight years after my analysis with her had ended and after a further two years with another woman analyst, began to learn what skills I may possess as a therapist from Irene.

By then my research project in Athens had finished and I was working as a psychiatric registrar at Horton Hospital, Epsom, while preparing to sit examinations for the Diploma of Psychological Medicine, a necessary *rite de passage* to full psychiatric qualification in the days before the Royal College of Psychiatrists had been founded. At Horton, fate was again kind to me. My immediate boss was the eminent forensic psychiatrist Henry Rollin, who was then deputy physician superintendent of the hospital. Henry and I quickly became, and remained, firm friends. A brilliant diagnostician and patient teacher, he gave me a secure grounding in general psychiatry and passed on to me the expertise necessary to understand and treat the most disturbed and challenging of patients. His lively personality and rich sense of humour meant that working at Horton was great fun as well as highly instructive. It was the sort of experience I could wish for any budding psychotherapist as a practical means to knowing the terrible extremes to which human nature can be pushed.

From 1968 until her death in 1976, Irene and I shared consulting rooms in London and, as she had done with Godwin Baynes, had regular discussions about the patients we were treating. During this period I was also analysing the mountains of data I had brought back with me from Greece and had embarked on an intensive reading of Jung's *Collected Works*. I obtained my DPM in 1969 and in the following year withdrew from the NHS into private practice. Though I continued to do some general psychiatry, and provided Irene and some other lay analysts with their psychiatric 'cover', I committed myself increasingly to my first love, analysis.

Of all that I learned during that apprenticeship, the most valuable was the realization that beneath the personal intelligence of everyone there is a deeper intelligence at work, which is the *evolved* intelligence of humankind. Through Irene I learned that the most effective way of mobilizing this intelligence is working with dreams.

Though analysis of the transference is important, it is only part of the process, and can be anti-therapeutic when it is made the primary focus of treatment. What is of crucial importance is the quality of the therapeutic alliance and collaborative work with the unconscious as manifested in dreams. I went on doing my best to work in this way thereafter, and I attempted to condense this experience in my book, *Private Myths: Dreams and Dreaming* (first published in 1995).

Enter Michael Fordham

When Irene went to work with Godwin Baynes, he was writing *Mythology of the Soul,* and they spent many hours discussing the paintings and dreams of a physician on whose analysis the first half of the book is based. The physician concerned was to have a powerful impact on the development of Jungian psychology in England and, eventually, in the United States. His name was Michael Fordham (1905–1995).

A decisive event in Michael Fordham's history, in Baynes's view, was the death of his mother when he was twelve. This trauma, combined with the personality of his detached, intellectually erratic father (who devoted himself to Fabian political enthusiasms and to the arts and crafts movement rather than to the emotional needs of his bereft son) resulted in a one-sided, inhibited development, which Baynes did not hesitate to diagnose as schizoid.

Fordham later confirmed this opinion in the autobiography he wrote towards the end of his life:

> School life began well, but after my mother's death and the disintegration of family life, it changed. I did not realize why at the time but I knew later that I had split and that my emotional life had gone underground. (Fordham, 1994, p. 46).

Baynes described Fordham as proceeding through life like an

automaton among automata:

> He saw that experiences which moved other men meant nothing to him. Instead of being fluid and adaptable, his feeling was withdrawn and unready. From the time of his mother's death there seems to have been a certain withdrawal or introversion of personal feeling. Charm of manner made him acceptable, but psychologically he lived in chilly isolation.

Coming from an ancient clan of East Anglian farmers, Fordham was educated at Gresham's School, Holt (where he was a contemporary of W. H. Auden and the embarrassed recipient of a love poem from him), and Trinity College, Cambridge. He studied medicine at St Bartholomew's Hospital, and would have become a neurologist were it not for his early marriage to Molly Swaby when he was 23. Shortage of money forced him to accept an appointment as a junior medical officer at Long Grove Hospital, a mental hospital close to Horton, where I was to be employed more than thirty years later.

There he began reading Jung. Fordham was at first sceptical about Jung's theory of the collective unconscious, but he nevertheless decided to put it to the test. One of his Long Grove patients believed himself to be 'the devil's disciple'. The evil that had him in its power was rotting away his internal organs, and his eventual death, he declared, would take away the sins of humanity. If Jung was right, Fordham reasoned, then this unfortunate patient was in the grip of some scapegoat myth and he should be able to find comparable details in Frazer's *The Golden Bough*. Sure enough, the themes apparent in the patient's delusions were all there.

Fordham's experience of mental hospital work does not seem to have been as happy or rewarding as mine. He was not an easy man to get on with, and, having fallen out with his colleagues and his physician superintendent Dr F. G. L. Barnes, he left Long Grove to work at the London Child Guidance Clinic. Although, as he acknowledged, Fordham had 'no special liking for children', he found the clinical work interesting. At first he understood the behaviour disorders and neuroses of his patients to be a function of unconscious conflicts in their parents. Such an approach accorded with Jung's view that child analysis could achieve little and could do actual harm if the parents' problems were left untreated.

As he gained experience, however, Fordham felt a need to intervene more actively in his work with children. He came to see a child's psyche less as a passive reflection of parental influences and more as a dynamic entity with its own priorities and agendas. Adapting some features of his own analysis with Baynes, he encouraged children to recount their dreams, draw and paint their inner images, and take pleasure in fairy tales. As a result of this imaginative approach, Fordham began to build up a reputation for the treatment of severely disturbed children.

Feeling a need for more extensive psychological understanding, Fordham went, on Baynes's suggestion, to Zurich to seek an analytic training with Jung. He wrote to Jung explaining that his financial resources were low and that he would have to support himself by finding work in Switzerland. He drew all his funds out of the bank to pay for the journey and his hotel. When he presented himself in Zurich, however, he was told by Jung that the Swiss authorities, fearing a massive influx of refugees, had made it virtually impossible for foreigners to work there. 'As I went back to England I became very angry', wrote Fordham in his memoir *The Making of an Analyst* (1994). 'How could he drag me out to Zurich when he knew that my proposition was impossible; he must be seriously out of touch with human requirements or feelings!' Fordham was to remain ambivalent about Jung for the rest of his life. According to Vera von der Heydt, Irene, Barbara Hannah and several other members of the generation who knew Jung well, it was an ambivalence which Jung reciprocated, though he was later to propose Fordham as one of the three editors of the English translation of his *Collected Works*.

On his return to England after this fruitless journey, Fordham resumed his analysis with Baynes, and his work in child guidance. It was then that he turned to the work of Melanie Klein. He read *The Psycho-Analysis of Children*, he tells us, 'with amazement and emotional shock'. He was particularly impressed by Klein's use of play as a means of communication, by her belief in the basic role of fantasy in a child's development, and by her insistence that children invariably develop a transference to their therapist.

Fordham became particularly interested in the transference phenomenon, and this made him critical of Baynes's handling of his own analysis. Moreover, he had started an extra-marital affair, which Baynes encouraged him to continue as a means to making a conscious relationship with his anima. Fordham blamed him for this: 'His support contributed to the undermining of my marriage.' He also began to feel trapped in the analysis. Because he could not afford to pay fees, Baynes had agreed to accept Fordham's analytical material as payment, for inclusion in *Mythology of the Soul*. 'One disadvantage of this,' commented Fordham, 'was that I felt obliged to keep on producing pictures to keep up payments!' As his relationship with his wife deteriorated, he convinced himself that it was due to the absence of transference analysis in his work with Baynes.

Uncertain what to do, he asked to see Jung when he was next on a lecturing visit to London. It was characteristic of Jung's easy informality that he received him in his bedroom where he was dressing for dinner. When Fordham told him that he was finding it difficult with Baynes, Fordham thought he heard Jung mutter, 'Yes, I bet it is!' Then he said clearly: 'I saw at once that [Baynes] was identified with your material and if you want to do so you had better get out.'

Fordham followed Jung's advice, acknowledging, nevertheless, that his work with Baynes had been far from unproductive. It had released his imaginative powers, convinced him of the reality of unconscious processes and inspired him to go his own way in seeking his own professional destiny.

For a while he analysed with another Jungian, Hilde Kirsch, to whom he felt powerfully attracted, but he thought she also ducked the erotic nature of his transference and failed in her duty to him by declining to analyse it. Since, in his view, neither Baynes nor Kirsch knew how to analyse his childhood or understood how to work with transference, Fordham felt impelled to make these two aspects of analysis his particular concern. Here again we find another example of how the personal psychology of a creative individual can shape the analytic discipline he goes on to found.

During the war, having divorced Molly and married Frieda Hoyle (with whom he declared he rediscovered the sort of love he had had for his mother), Fordham was appointed to a consultant post created to help evacuee children in Nottinghamshire who had not been able to settle in billets. He seized this as a further opportunity to extend Jungian theory into childhood. Since his charges had been removed from their homes, their parents were not available for treatment and Fordham had, *faute de mieux*, to work on their internal representatives in the children's psyches through the medium of the transference.

On the basis of this experience, he published his first book *The Life of Childhood* in 1944. He reaffirmed that the Self, in the Jungian sense, was an active factor in child development and rejected the idea that disturbed children could only be treated indirectly. Children showed a remarkable capacity to overcome their difficulties, if given sympathetic understanding and support.

Godwin Baynes died of a cerebral tumour in 1943 and Fordham was to assume his mantle as the leading British Jungian for the next 50 years, founding with others the Society of Analytical Psychology (SAP) in 1946; the *Journal of Analytical Psychology* in 1955; and, together with Gerhard Adler, Herbert Read and William McGuire, producing the English edition of the *Collected Works* of C. G. Jung. In addition, Fordham wrote numerous articles and published eight books.

Although his contributions gave rise to much controversy and dissent, Fordham has to be acknowledged as one of the last analysts

41

in the twentieth century who, by the force of his own personality, was able to influence the course of analytic theory and practice. He saw himself as an innovator who corrected deficiencies in Jung's theoretical legacy by laying stress on the importance of transference and countertransference interactions between analyst and patient, and on the influence of infantile wishes and defences on the later development of the personality. Pursuing this line, he advocated a rapprochement between Jungian theories and those of the neo-Freudian, Kleinian and object relations schools of analysis. For these innovations he was applauded by some, but condemned by others who accused him of leading a regression to Freud's couch-oriented, reductive analytic techniques and of betraying the crea-tive-symbolic approach to personal development at the heart of classical Jungian practice.

But to many who wished to train as analytical psychologists in England, Fordham's amalgam of Jungian and Kleinian theories, augmented by his own observations and formulations concerning psychological development in infancy and childhood, were to prove attractive. By enshrining these principles in the training program offered by the SAP, Fordham exerted an influence over the practice of Jungian psychology not only in Britain but also in the United States.

Schisms

However, these developments did not meet with unqualified ac-claim. In the 1950s, a growing number of critics complained that Fordham's theoretical revisions had contributed to a crisis of identi-ty among members of the SAP, who began to question whether they could describe themselves as Jungian analysts at all. Gerhard Adler, one of Fordham's co-editors of Jung's *Collected Works,* who was analysed by Jung in the 1930s, felt so strongly that Fordham had deviated from the original spirit of Jung's work that, together with other analysts trained in Zurich, he set up an 'alternative train-ing' within the SAP. The conflict which ensued between these two theoretical orientations proved too intense for them to be contained

42

within the same organization. The 'orthodox' Zurich-oriented analysts eventually seceded to form their own Association of Jungian Analysts (AJA). This was itself to give birth to another 'classical' group with even closer ties to Zurich—the Independent Group of Analytical Psychologists (IGAP). The British Association of Psychotherapists (BAP), which offered both a Freudian and a Jungian (though SAP-biased) training, also arose.

There were those who maintained that the existence of no less than four Jungian training groups in London was due to Fordham's revision of Jungian psychology and his attempt to put a neo-Kleinian stamp on it. However, it is in the nature of analytic groups, of whatever school, to split on doctrinal grounds; and there is justice in Fordham's argument that analytical techniques, if they are to gain wide acquiescence, should be based on empirical observation. Accordingly, on Fordham's insistence, the training program of the SAP encourages candidates training as adult analysts (and requires all those training as child analysts) to devote time to the systematic observation of infants and young children. The SAP has continued to flourish and is now one of the largest and most influential Jungian societies in the world.

Fordham regarded the original split between Freud and Jung in 1913 as 'a disaster from which analytical psychology and psychoanalysis both suffer and will continue to suffer until the damage is repaired'. He devoted his life to attempting to effect this repair but in the process succeeded in generating further splits, which resembled in their intensity and animosity the split between the Freudians and the Kleinians.

The problem about reconciling differences between groups embracing differing ideologies is that people become so deeply wedded to their belief systems as to feel wholly identified with them. As a result, any attempt to persuade them to relinquish or modify their beliefs is experienced as an assault on their personal security. Their response, then, is to band together with like-minded colleagues and look to their defences. Moreover, as studies of religious cults reveal, the more irrational the belief system and the more it lacks empirical foundation, the more loyal its adherents and the more hostile they become to those who hold contrary opinions. In analytic societies this loyalty to group beliefs is intensified by the training analysis, whose purpose is to ensure that candidates do not merely learn their theories and techniques but integrate them as indispensable components of their entire personality.

One may respect Fordham's efforts to extend analytic understanding of the role played by the Self in early childhood development but, with hindsight, we can see that in carrying Jungian psychology in a Kleinian direction he had taken a wrong turning. It would have been scientifically more productive and theoretically more compatible with the corpus of Jungian theory, if instead he had turned towards Bowlby and attachment theory. Fordham sometimes wrote as if he were the only analyst to hold that the child was no tabula rasa but an intact individual full of innate human potential, who influenced and moulded the environment as much as the environment influenced and moulded her or him. But, as was indicated in the last chapter of Volume 2, this position was proposed and developed to much more systematic and influential effect by Bowlby and Mary Ainsworth, whose carefully framed hypotheses concerning child development have given rise to much valuable research and many therapeutic initiatives throughout the world. Yet, in his books, Fordham omitted all mention of Bowlby and the important consequences of his work.

Not surprisingly, attempts made by younger, more progressive analysts to bring the four individual Jungian groups in London under a general 'Umbrella Group' encountered major problems in trying to heal the split between the Fordhamite and classical wings. What, then, was the split about, and what were the main characteristics of the two approaches? In his influential book *Jung and the Post-Jungians* (1985), Andrew Samuels summarized these differences under four headings: use of the couch; frequency of sessions; the use of reductive interpretations as opposed to amplification; the more passive versus the more active participation of the analyst in the analytic relationship.

Whereas Jung abandoned the couch to facilitate mutuality between analyst and patient, Fordham reverted to its use. Classical Jungians found this reversion unacceptable because they argued the couch got in the way of the therapeutic alliance, emphasized the patient's passivity, and encouraged a retreat from the real world into a regressive infantile state of dependency. Fordham's supporters countered that the couch stressed the fact that the analysand is a patient, that analysis is a formal procedure, and that it facilitates the recovery of infantile fantasies that provide vital analytic material.

With regard to the frequency of sessions, Fordham's followers insisted that at least four sessions a week were necessary if the procedure was to be called 'analysis'. Any fewer sessions must be regarded as mere 'psychotherapy'. However, this was a circular definition of analysis which completely left out of account what actually goes on in an 'analytic' session. Jung's position on this was quite clear: 'In my experience', he wrote, 'the absolute period of cure is not shortened by too many sittings. It lasts a fair time in all cases requiring thorough treatment' (*CW* 17, para. 43). Contemporary outcome studies provide no evidence to contradict him. Classical Jungians contend that analysis essentially consists of working with unconscious material (whether in dreams, fantasies, symbols, or transference phenomena), irrespective of the number of sessions per week. Most 'classical' practitioners see their patients once or twice a week.

The third major difference between the two camps was one of emphasis: the Fordhamites indulging more in reductive interpretations of their patient's material, whereas the classical Jungians made greater use of amplification (i.e., educing mythic, historical, and cultural parallels to 'amplify' the material, enabling patients to reach beyond their purely personal associations so as to relate them to a wider human context). In part, this distinction reflected Freud's pessimism as opposed to Jung's therapeutic optimism: the reductive view sees the glass half empty, whereas the synthetic view sees the glass half full. Jung again:

> The analytical reductive view asserts that interest (libido) streams back regressively to infantile reminiscences and there "fixates"—if indeed it has ever freed itself from them. The synthetic or anagogic view, on the contrary, asserts that certain parts of the personality which are capable of development are in an infantile state, as though still in the womb. Both interpretations can be shown to be correct. We might almost say that they amount virtually to the same thing. But it makes an enormous difference in practice whether we interpret something regressively or progressively. (*CW* 17, para. 9)

A further important distinction arose here: whereas Fordham stated that 'interpretation is the cornerstone of analytic technique', classical Jungians found the very notion of 'technique' or 'interpretation' objectionable for a number of reasons. Firstly, it put the analyst in a position of power, encouraging him or her to impose their dogmatic preconceptions on the patient; secondly, it inhibited the autonomous flow of psychic images and the honouring of new symbols as they emerged; and, finally, it negated Jung's conception of analysis as an art.

The fourth difference concerned the analyst's conduct: whereas Fordham advocated the Freudian model of reticence, waiting for the patient to produce material to which the analyst may or may not respond; the classical analyst was and still is more willing to contribute to the dialogue and draw on his own knowledge of symbolism to amplify the patient's material. Since, for the classical Jungian, a session is a social occasion as well as a therapeutic encounter, more emphasis is placed on the therapeutic alliance than on the use of transference and countertransference. Not only does there exist good empirical evidence in support of this emphasis, but some psychoanalysts started to come round to a similar position. For example, Heinz Kohut (1977), with his stress on the importance of empathy, abandoned the neutral 'reticent and reserved' model: 'To remain silent when one is asked a question', he said, 'is not neutral but rude.'

In view of the radical differences that exist between these two positions, it would be extraordinary if the Umbrella Group had succeeded in transcending them. Its work was not made any easier by the formal creation of two much bigger official bodies, whose function it was to regulate the psychotherapeutic profession in such a way as to prepare its members for legal registration. These were the United Kingdom Council for Psychotherapy (UKCP), now consisting of over 7,000 members, and the smaller British Confederation of Psychotherapists (BCP), which split off from the UKCP in 1992, and subsequently reestablished itself as the British Psychoanalytic Council (BPC).

Whereas the UKCP incorporates members from a host of different psychotherapeutic bodies (75 of them at the latest count), the BPC is an exclusive club restricted to fifteen member organizations and five affiliate member institutions drawn from psychoanalysis, psychoanalytic psychotherapy and analytical psychology. Psychoanalysts made up the majority of the original BCP members, and it was these neo-Freudians and Kleinians who led the move to establish their own Athenaeum out of a distaste for having to rub shoulders with the great unwashed of the UKCP. This has caused further friction between the four Jungian groups for, whereas the two Fordhamite groups were permitted to join the BCP, the two 'classical' groups were not—mainly because they were regarded as 'unsound' on the issues of frequency of sessions and analysis of the transference (Casement, 1995).

The main preoccupation of the BCP was with 'standards'. This is understandable. When a group embraces a system of belief and practice which is not empirically based or verifiable, it necessarily becomes rigid over the matter of rules and regulations. Thus, the BCP became obsessional about the number of analytic sessions per week conducted by analysts, trainees and trainees working with clinical patients, insisting on an absolute minimum of three-times-a-week as necessary for positive outcome in treatment. And there is

47

good reason to suppose that, with the decline in psychoanalytic repute, practitioners who insist on three or four or five times-a-week will price themselves out of a dwindling market.

Thus, the whole question of frequency of sessions may well become less a matter of ideology than of economics. Increasingly, analysts on both sides of the Atlantic are experiencing difficulty in finding enough patients willing to pay for more than one or two sessions a week for a treatment that is by no means certain of producing the profound and lasting therapeutic results they would wish for. There is growing evidence that psychoanalysts and Fordhamite Jungians are having to compromise and become increasingly flexible on this issue.

Andrew Samuels (2008), for example, is particularly up-beat about this, maintaining that many Jungian practitioners have by now internalized the debate between the classical and Fordhamite approaches, and that they 'feel perfectly capable of functioning as either a classical or a developmental or an archetypal psychologist according to the needs of the individual analysand. Or the analyst may regard his or her orientation as primarily classical, for example, but with a flourishing developmental component, or some other combination.'

Signs that the neo-Freudians and other members of the British Psychoanalytic Council are moving in the same direction may be deduced from the Strategic Vision document that they circulated in October 2011. This argued for the acceptance of organizations 'whose members train and work at lower frequencies', and advocated closer collaboration with other counselling and psychotherapeutic organizations so as to 'develop a comprehensive and diverse training infrastructure throughout the UK'. This initiative has occurred as a defensive response to the British Government's 'Improving Access to Psychological Therapies' program, which is exclusively concerned with providing 'evidence based psychotherapies, as approved by the National Institute for Health and Clinical Excellence (NICE), for people with depression and anxiety disorders'. Practitioners of Cognitive Behaviour Therapy are the main beneficiaries of this program, and it has placed under threat those services that provide long-term analytically orientated psycho-therapy, many of which are having to close down as a result. Research-driven compromise is now the order of the day and the BPC appears to be fighting for its life.

The evolutionary dimension

The battles which raged throughout the 1970s between the different Jungian groups left me unaffected because I did not belong to any of them. As a qualified psychiatrist and medical practitioner, I was free to treat my patients as I wished, using whatever procedures I considered best suited to their needs. Every week I spent three days in London and four days at my home in Devon. Though I continued to do some general psychiatry, my practice was predominantly analytic. In cheerful accordance with Jung's advice (having carefully prepared my patients beforehand), I took long breaks every year, usually in Samos or Crete, where it was possible to rent a seaside cottage for the equivalent of about three pounds ($4.50) a week. There for three glorious months I would enjoy a sense of total freedom—to read, ponder and write, swim, walk in the mountains; enjoy the delights of Greek food and retsina, and—best of all—the company of Greek friends.

Intellectually, the 1970s were a challenging and creative time for me. Irene died of cancer in 1976, leaving me her library which included all the volumes so far published of Jung's *Collected Works*. I grieved for her and was professionally very much on my own. But, largely thanks to her, I had a flourishing practice and was finding my feet as an analyst in a way that Jung would probably have approved. For he resisted the foundation of an Institute of Analytical Psychology until almost the end of his life, and agreed to it then because, as he said, 'They'll only set up one up between my death and my funeral', and he felt it might be as well if he had a hand in the form that it took. The last thing he wanted was to shackle his followers with the bureaucracy and the kind of doctrinal orthodoxy imposed by Freud on the Freudians.

As Freud's reputation declined, the authoritarian grip exerted by psychoanalytic institutes tightened, if anything, as is well described by Stephen Frosh, Reader in Psychoanalytical Psychology at Birkbeck College and a consultant at the Tavistock Clinic. In his book *For and Against Psychoanalysis* (1998), Frosh described how training to become a psychoanalyst in the British Psycho-Analytical Society consisted of passing time under the critical scrutiny of authority figures, and several years of five-times-a-week personal analysis plus the management of two five-times-a-week cases under weekly supervision. Frosh wrote:

> Given the enormous investment of time and money in the training, particularly the personal analysis, plus the exposure of one's own secret longings, impulses and failures to the scrutiny of someone who, until the very last minute, is in a position to refuse a trainee entry into the professional society, it would not be surprising if what was produced were dogmatic, conformist and scared neophytes unable to challenge any of the received wisdom to which they have been exposed.

This is the kind of tyranny that is prone to occur when a society coheres round a corpus of doctrine and belief not susceptible to empirical verification: it employs the well-tested processes of indoctrination characteristic of a totalitarian state, rather than the non-coercive give-and-take one would hope to find in an association of enlightened professionals.

I am thankful that my own peculiar development as an analyst enabled me to escape such intellectual subjugation, though I am naturally aware that analysts who have put themselves through such initiatory torments will regard me as hopelessly untrained—not least because my 'training cases' were supervised by the person who had been my analyst, a practice which is nowadays considered distinctly bad form. However, not having to stick to an official curriculum, I was free to read widely in ethology, mythology, anthropology, Freudian psychology and object relations theory; as well as Jung's *Collected Works*, which, like Shakespeare's plays or Beethoven's quartets, yield greater rewards every time one returns to them.

Intrigued by the striking parallels between Jung and the ethologists, I began writing my first book, *Archetypes: A Natural History of the Self*, which was eventually published in 1982 (a revised edition, *Archetype Revisited: An Updated Natural History of the Self* was published in 2002) This was an attempt to bring together all the strands of my experience up to that point so as to integrate the analyst in me with the psychiatrist and the experimental psychologist.

Standing outside the professional organizations, with their political agendas and mutual hostilities, and unhampered by any doctrinal allegiances, I felt free to explore the evolutionary implications of archetypal theory in such fundamental areas as the formation of attachment bonds between adults and between parents and children; the development of the personality through the course of the life-cycle; the role of religious practices and initiation rites in incorporating individuals within their community; the role of the shadow personality in causing hostility between individuals, groups and nations; the pathological consequences of thwarting archetypal needs or intentions; and so on. As I wrote it, there developed in me the desire to share in the creation of a humane science of human nature that would embrace psychology, anthropology, psychoanalysis, psychiatry and medicine within the ambit of evolutionary theory. Such an achievement could ultimately transcend the doctrinal differences between warring analytic factions by opening up their formulations and practices to empirical investigation and by putting them on a sound epistemological base.

Though the book sold well in Britain and the United States and many Jungians expressed polite appreciation, few appeared to share my enthusiasm for the biological aspects of Jung's thinking, ostensibly because such concerns seemed irrelevant to what they did in their consulting rooms. Jungian psychology had done pretty well

51

without an interest in evolution up to then, so what was the point?

What was more hurtful was that some also accused me of being 'reductive', of trying to turn Jung into some kind of Darwinian fundamentalist. To have one's intentions so completely misunderstood is a painful experience and I pondered its cause and came to the conclusion that it was largely due to the fact that most contemporary Jungians, unlike Jung himself, have not had a medical or biological training, but instead have studied subjects such as the humanities, theology or the social sciences in universities where the standard social science model (which strictly eschews biology) still prevails. Jung would not have been happy about this. He was keen that his pupils should, when possible, complete a medical training before they began analyzing with him. For example, he wouldn't take on Joe Henderson or Joe Wheelright (both destined to become celebrated Californian analysts) unless they first became doctors, which they dutifully did.

I am not suggesting that the absence of a medical degree diminishes the effectiveness of a Jungian analyst as a therapist. Quite the contrary. Most of the best analysts of my experience have had no medical training at all, but for some it requires an extra effort of the imagination to appreciate the crucial contribution that biological science can make to the survival of analytical psychology as an intact and self-perpetuating discipline.

It was, I suppose, inevitable that my own training in psychology, medicine, neurology, psychiatry and biology would have led me to focus on the biological pole of the archetype, but this did not mean that I was any less concerned with the spiritual pole, as I hope my books on dreams (1995) and symbols (1998) clearly demonstrate.

There was one more factor with uncomfortable implications: the hideous perversion of Darwinism practised by the Nazis has given rise to an understandable wariness throughout the post-war Western world about the application of biological science to the study of human psychology and behaviour. A historically inspired misunderstanding of the essentially neutral, non-political nature of biology (*bios* = life: the study of life) has been the unfortunate result.

Some hostile criticisms resurfaced in reviews of *Evolutionary Psychiatry: A New Beginning* (2000) which I wrote with the evolutionary psychiatrist, John Price. I will respond to these caveats in Chapter 3, but at this juncture I would make the point that what I am truly concerned about is the survival of what I perceive to be of greatest value in Jung's achievement, and for this reason my primary concern has been with epistemology—the foundations of psychological knowledge. Why do we believe what we believe about human psychology, and how do we know that it is true? This has become the crucial issue for all schools of psychoanalysis in the second century of their existence.

The two widely acclaimed books by Richard Noll (1994; 1997) sought to prove that Jungian psychology was a mere religious cult geared to an exploitative capitalist enterprise and that Jungian theory was without any basis or value. Noll alleged that the evidence Jung advanced in support of the theory of archetypes was entirely fraudulent and wholly incompatible with biological science. Judging from the enthusiasm with which these books were received in the press—the first (*The Jung Cult*) won the 'Best Book of the Year' award of the American Association of Publishers—this was what a large number of people wanted to hear.

So why do Jungians hold to the principles, theories, beliefs and practices that they do? The public, no less than the academics, are going to require evidence. The justification, 'Dr Jung said it was so', will no longer be sufficient. This is why epistemology has become the essential issue for analytical psychology at this time in its history and why it is important, when evolutionary theory is beginning to play a central role in psychological and psychiatric thinking, to examine the biological implications of archetypal theory. Jung corrected, deepened and extended Freud's intention to make psychoanalysis a science compatible with biology.

Instead of conceiving the psyche as the product of postulated drives and conflicts, Jung saw it as a richly adaptive consequence of the evolution of the human species. He may have had some curious notions about how precisely that evolution occurred, but his commitment to the ideas of evolution, metamorphosis, growth and development was apparent in nearly everything he wrote.

What is most profoundly important is Jung's concept of the Self as the central organizing principle of the personality, maintaining a state of homeostatic balance between conscious and unconscious forces, guiding the individual through the stages of life from the cradle to the grave. It is infinitely richer in its implications than the self postulated by neo-Freudians like Donald Winnicott (1965) and Heinz Kohut (1971) who view the self as something created in the course of personal development and not as an archetypal 'given' rooted in the evolutionary history of the species, which itself guides and influences the course of human life span.

Much psychoanalytic theory-building is imaginatively architectural. But the structures so erected are generally castles in the air— spectral concretizations of their creators' personal fantasies. Too often the theoretical bricks used in their construction are reified and treated as if they were real. The purpose of the training analysis, then, becomes to sustain the illusion through succeeding generations of practitioners. Many intelligent laypersons, outside the analytic fraternities, have always suspected this. Public skepticism about the value of analysis, combined with reluctance on the part of governments, hospital trusts and medical insurance companies to pay for such an expensive, open-ended and uncertain treatment, has meant that analytical theories and procedures have increasingly come under critical scrutiny. As a result, the different analytic traditions will have to agree on the basic principles that they all share, and render their activities more accountable to systematic evaluation.

However, each therapeutic approach develops its own value system or 'culture', which is attractive to some people and repellent to others. It would be a misfortune if these cultural differences were lost under the grey imposition of bureaucratic uniformity. Psycho-therapy is such an intimate procedure; and the personality, attitudes and values of the therapist are so decisive as to outcome, that there will always be a place for different philosophical traditions—however much scientific agreement may emerge about the basic characteristics of human nature. Often, in the actual therapeutic encounter, wisdom becomes more important than science. While the theories on which analysis is based should be scientifically grounded, the practice of analysis is, and will always remain, an art.

At the present state of knowledge, therefore, the kind of therapy one chooses to submit to as a prospective patient, or the analytic association one seeks to join as a trainee analyst, must be a matter of taste rather than scientific reasoning. Given the nature of my own 'personal equation', it is understandable that, by and large, my sympathies should lie with the classical Jungians; and when, in the mid-1980s, the Independent Group of Analytical Psychologists kindly invited me to join them, I was pleased to accept, not least because of my awareness that, given my idiosyncratic background, they were probably the only group that would have me. Unlike Groucho Marx, I was glad to join a club that would have me as a member! This in no way reflects adversely on the other members of IGAP, who include some of the most distinguished analysts in Britain; but that they are willing to tolerate me is in accordance with their thoroughly independent philosophy.

Personally, I believe that Jung's contribution to the world of analysis has been of incalculable importance because of his open-mindedness, his broad humanity, and his profound insight into the human condition. His temperamental antipathy to reductionism, institutionalism and the imposition of rigid orthodoxy is deeply attractive, and in stressing the evolutionary implications of his thought I have no desire to reverse what George Hogenson has called Jung's 'radical empiricism' in order to implicate him in some form of Darwinian fundamentalism. As Jung himself put it:

We keep forgetting that we are primates and that we have to make allowances for these primitive layers in our psyche. ... Individuation is not only an upward but also a downward process. Without any body, there is no mind and therefore no individuation. (McGuire, 1977).

For Jung, the psyche was primary, more important than anything else, since it was only through the psyche that we could know anything or feel anything at all. However much we may come to know about how the brain works and how genes influence our behaviour, it is in our psyches that we shall continue to live.

It was in teaching the art of moblizing psychic potential that Jung was an unsurpassed master. Most important is his emphasis on the supremely personal nature of analysis and the need for the analyst to go on growing:

> The analyst must go on learning endlessly, and never forget that each new case brings problems to light and thus gives rise to unconscious assumptions that have never before been constellated. We could say, without too much exaggeration, that a good half of every treatment that probes at all deeply consists in the doctor's examining himself, for only what he can put right in himself can he hope to put right in the patient. It is no loss, either, if he feels that the patient is hitting him, or even scoring off him: it is his own hurt that gives the measure of his power to heal. This, and nothing else, is the meaning of the Greek myth of the wounded physician. (*CW* 16, para. 239).

As a new science of evolutionary psychotherapy begins to emerge, it will need to be practised in this quintessentially Jungian spirit if it is to be truly humane.

2
RESEARCH

It has to be acknowledged that a lot is still not understood about how or why therapy works, when it works and for whom it works. Whatever therapists may say about what they do or why they do it, the fact of the matter is that the origins of their therapeutic beliefs and practices are derived, ultimately, from magic.

As in the remote past, patients come to therapists in search of a miraculous cure. This is why the most successful schools have grown up round a charismatic founder of impressive personal authority. From Father Gassner's public exorcism of hysterical nuns in 1775, Anton Mesmer's therapeutic successes in Vienna and Paris in the 1780s, Justinus Kerner's treatment of the Seeress of Prevorst (and the immensely successful book he wrote about it—the first detailed study of one psychiatric patient, and the first systematic record of the extraordinary myth-making capacities of the unconscious), to Charcot's dramatic induction and removal of hysterical paralyses at the Salpêtrière using hypnosis, and Breuer and Freud's (spurious) cure of Anna O. through the talking treatment … all this grew out of the ancient theory and practice of exorcism. The notion of unconscious motivation, the use of free association, the interpretation of dreams and the analysis of the transference, are modern attempts to apply these principles in a rational manner, but we are still largely ignorant of the underlying processes.

That the different schools of therapy, founded on the assumptions of their charismatic leaders, have developed into exclusive 'sects' is because these assumptions have largely escaped objective verification. In the absence of sound empirical foundations, each school has attempted to make good the deficiency by establishing strictly 'professional' credentials, with strict rules and regulations of varying degrees of practical relevance about how therapy should be done. These regulations have sometimes attained obsessive-compulsive rigidity—the number of times a week patients must be seen; whether or not they should be greeted, touched, or helped on with their coats; whether they should continue to pay for their sessions when they or their analysts are on holiday; and so on. The furious arguments that have characterized the proceedings of the United Kingdom Council for Psychotherapy have largely centred round such arcane details, and the impasse that results is attributable to the lack of reliable evidence concerning the relative success or failure of these different therapeutic approaches. If a way is to be found, out of this confusion, then well-conducted research could provide the key.

For the first half of the twentieth century no systematic attempt was made to assess the outcome of psychoanalytic treatment. But then in 1952, Hans Eysenck, Professor of Psychology at London University, caused a sensation by producing statistics that seemed to demonstrate that psychoanalysis did no good whatsoever. His initial onslaught was followed by a further attack in 1965. Quoting more statistics, Eysenck tried to show that neurotic patients who received psychoanalysis were no better off after two years of treatment than comparable patients who received no treatment at all.

However, in the bitter controversies that ensued, doubt was thrown on Eysenck's interpretation of the data available to him. More rigorous research followed, the results broadly supporting the claim of psychodynamic therapists that their efforts were effective. In 1970, Meltzoff and Kornreich published a careful and much quoted survey of one hundred research projects and concluded that the benefits of psychotherapy were established beyond all reasonable doubt. But Eysenck remained unconvinced. The only valid form of treatment in his view was behaviour therapy, because it was based on the scientifically verifiable principles of Pavlovian conditioning. This assertion caused a further row, this time between the psychoanalysts and the behaviourists, which engendered some interesting research designed to compare the results of these two methods of treatment.

One such investigation was that of R. B. Sloane and his colleagues, published in 1975. They studied three groups consisting of 30 neurotics in each group: one group received psychodynamic therapy, another received behaviour therapy, and the third group was kept on the waiting list. The members of all three groups were thoroughly assessed at the beginning of the program, again after four months and again one year later. A number of individuals improved or recovered in all three groups, although the people who received treatment in the two treated groups did significantly better than those in the control group who languished in limbo on the waiting list and received no treatment at all.

An interesting finding, not well received by the analysts, was the absence of any significant difference between the improvements displayed by the group that had had behaviour therapy and the group treated by psychodynamic therapy. Later research yielded similar findings. Predictably, the psychoanalysts explained the success of the behaviourists in terms of the transference, while the behaviourists explained the psychoanalytic successes in terms of their own learning theories.

But having established that some form of psychotherapy was better than no therapy at all, researchers turned their attention to what precisely it was that contributed to psychotherapeutic success. Fairly general agreement emerged that, contrary to the assertions of Freudians and Kleinians, lengthy analysis of the transference and detailed unravelling of Oedipal and castration anxieties were not indispensable to favourable outcome.

Recent findings are in tune with these conclusions and the past two decades have seen publication of a number of authoritative, not to say 'magisterial', reviews such as *Psychodynamic Treatment Research* edited by N. E. Miller and colleagues (1993), *Handbook of Psychotherapy and Behavioural Change* (Fifth edition) edited by Allen E. Bergin and Sol L. Garfield (2004), *Research Foundations for Psychotherapy Practice* edited by Mark Aveline and David Shapiro (1995), *What Works For Whom: A Critical Review of*

Psychotherapy Research by Anthony Roth and Peter Fonagy (2005) and *Essential Research Findings in Counselling and Psychotherapy* (2008) by Mick Cooper.

The work of Roth and Fonagy is of particular interest because of its scrupulous objectivity, written as it is by a cognitive therapist (Roth) and a professor of psychoanalysis (Fonagy). Reviewing the evidence for the efficacy of psychotherapy in the treatment of common psychiatric disorders such as depression, anxiety, eating disorders, personality disorders, sexual dysfunction and so on, they divide the different therapies available into those that have been demonstrated to be effective and those that have either proved to be promising or have received only limited support for their efficacy. On the whole, cognitive behavioural therapies fare best, while evidential support for psychodynamic therapies is harder to come by, though the authors repeatedly stress that lack of evidence does not necessarily mean that psychodynamic therapies are ineffective. In his Foreword to the 1996 edition of Roth and Fonagy's book, David Shapiro Professor of Clinical Psychology at the University of Leeds declared that the beliefs and claims of psychotherapists had been more critically and searchingly challenged than those of any other practitioners and that, by then, there had accumulated more and better scientific evidence to support the effectiveness of psychotherapy than many other interventions in health care at that time.

Much of this evidence comes from the use of 'meta-analysis', which compares findings from many hundreds or even thousands of different studies. However, Shapiro acknowledged that there had been relatively little progress in developing an evidence base for longer-term psychodynamic therapies. As Mick Cooper's invaluable book demonstrates, the extensive research of recent years has still failed to establish beyond doubt that one form of therapy is more effective than others across a range of different psychological disorders. The Dodo bird verdict still holds: everyone continues to win, and all get prizes.

Several explanations have been offered to account for this. One possibility is that the essential factors contributing to positive outcome may be common to all therapies, including psychoanalysis. Patients who have reported they benefited from therapy have attributed their improved condition to such factors as the reassuring comfort derived from forming a bond to a warm, accepting psychotherapist, the reduction in anxiety or despair afforded by the expectation of being helped, the gaining of some understanding of the nature of their problems, the acquisition of better-adjusted patterns of behaviour and the influence of the therapist's personality. A further crucial factor may well be the provision of a plausible system of explanation enabling patients to make sense of their situation.

Satisfaction of the need for explanations might indeed serve to explain the extraordinary cultural success of the entire therapeutic enterprise. The need for explanatory systems is apparent in all human societies, and accounts for the ubiquitous occurrence of mythic and religious explanations of the origins and nature of human existence. In our own culture Christianity is one example of such a system: Darwinism, Marxism and Freudianism are others. Up to the time of the ancient Greeks explanatory systems had been essentially mythic or magico-religious, expressed in terms of occult powers. In modern times, scientific explanations have banished hidden 'powers', replacing them with naturally occurring 'energy'. Freud's explanatory system fell somewhere between the mythic and the scientific, for he still clung to the notion of occult 'drives' operating in the unconscious.

Both Freud and Jung have been accused not only of founding 'cults', but of seeking to replace Judeo-Christianity with quasi-religious systems of their own devising. There is an element of truth in this, since the cultural vacuum left by the demise of Judeo-Christianity was demanding to be filled with something. In the last decade of the twentieth century it became apparent that Freudianism had failed as a satisfactory explanation in the West, as Marxism had in the East. Both retreated, leaving monetarism and scientific materialism as the primary explanatory systems ruling our cultural lives. For many people this is not enough. The explanatory vacuum remains. It is in this vacuum that psychotherapists continue to do their work.

Freud's constantly repeated claim that psychoanalysis was a science has not withstood the attacks of philosophers of science like Ernest Nagel, Sidney Hook and Karl Popper, who have demonstrated that psychoanalytic theory does not satisfy the most basic requirements of a true science, since the bungee-like flexibility of its postulates does not permit of their falsification. Given the most exhaustive case history, highly qualified and experienced psychoanalysts can produce conflicting but equally plausible interpretations of the same material, and no systematic method exists for establishing the validity of their alternative formulations; nor are they able to make accurate predictions about the patient's future mental state.

The scientific credibility of psychoanalysis stands or falls on Freud's 'tally argument'. The tally argument holds that a patient's condition will only improve if the interpretations offered by the analyst tally with the actual processes occurring within the patient. But, as Grünbaum pointed out in an influential book published in 1984 (*The Foundations of Psychoanalysis: A Philosophical Critique*), Freud's tally argument rests on the conjunction of two causally necessary conditions: that psychoanalysis can provide valid insights into the unconscious conflicts responsible for a neurosis, and that these insights are *indispensable* to curing the neurosis. Since, as recent research has shown, unique validity cannot be attributed to psychoanalytic insights and unique effectiveness cannot be claimed for psychoanalytic treatment, it follows, Grünbaum argued, that psychoanalysis must surrender its 'epistemic warrant' to scientific credibility.

As early as the 1960s, 'independent' psychoanalysts, such as Charles Rycroft, were arguing that psychoanalysis should cease to think of itself as a scientific discipline, but rather consider itself as a branch of the humanities, like literary criticism or biblical exegesis (from which the term *hermeneutics* is derived). Understandably, this 'hermeneutic perspective' has grown in popularity among psychoanalysts, since it would allow them to escape with some dignity from the uncomfortable realization that their work has no basis in science.

Laying the issue of scientific proof on one side, the hermeneutic approach holds that the value of a formulation can be derived from its coherence, consistency and narrative intelligibility, considered within the whole context of the patient's history in conjunction with data derived from the analytic situation. This rather begs the issue of who makes the judgement of coherence, consistency and intelligibility; and what determines the grounds for assessing the criteria on which the judgement is based.

A straight answer to the question 'Does psychoanalysis work in the way that psychoanalysts say it does?' is 'No, it doesn't.' Five-times-a-week treatment analysing the transference and counter-transference over a period of several years at very considerable cost produces no greater improvement than once a week 'supportive' therapy with a sympathetic nurse on the National Health. That, at any rate, is what research up to the present time would indicate. 'All that time and money', exclaimed Stephen Frosh (1998), 'all those complicated words and painful silences—and it does not even work.'

The research supporting this uncomfortable conclusion is not inconsiderable. One of the most impressive psychoanalytic studies was conducted by the Menninger Foundation which followed up patients over a period of up to 30 years (Wallerstein, 1986). Patients were given either psychoanalytic psychotherapy or supportive psychotherapy. They were seen by their therapists for as long as necessary: this varied between six months and 12 years from their initial assessment in the 1950s. All patients were followed up two or three years after termination of their treatment, and many remained in contact with the researchers for 12 to 24 years longer. Some were still receiving treatment 30 years later!

The most striking finding of what Frosh calls 'this remarkable and honourable study', was that it provided no evidence of any superior effect of psychoanalytic psychotherapy over supportive therapy. In fact, the outcome of psychoanalytic psychotherapy was worse, while that of supportive psychotherapy was better, than the investigators expected.

Other studies have produced similar results. In a review of outcome research in psychoanalysis published in 1995, Judy Kantrovitz summarized the results of six 'systematic clinical-quantitative studies of terminated analyses' that had been conducted over the previous decades. Altogether these involved 550 patients in four-or-five-times-a-week psychoanalysis conducted by supervised trainees at four psychoanalytic institutes. The findings of each of these studies were strikingly similar: while all patients received some therapeutic benefit for their neurotic difficulties, their improvement was not directly attributable to the specifically psychoanalytic aspects of their treatment.

These negative findings are all the more impressive when it is realized that the studies were mostly conducted by researchers well disposed to psychoanalysis, many being psychoanalysts themselves, and were therefore likely to be biased in the direction of producing positive results. It says much for the researchers' integrity that they reported their findings with such commendable objectivity. 'Still', commented Frosh, 'the point is that despite the failure of researchers wedded to psychoanalysis to demonstrate its effectiveness, the profession grinds on, its fees charged and paid, its training institutes still in demand.'

Some psychoanalysts have followed Charles Rycroft in responding to these negative findings by insisting that, since theirs is an interpretative or hermeneutic discipline unrelated to the physical sciences and logically distinct from them, their work cannot be subjected to scientific evaluation. However, this ingenuous argument completely overlooks the fact that psychoanalysts make the kind of statements about the pathological consequences of certain childhood events and about the positive outcomes of psychoanalytic treatment which *are* susceptible to scientific validation or refutation. The only escape from such scrutiny would be for psychoanalysis to give up all claims to therapeutic effectiveness and psychopathological explanation and become a branch of 'cultural studies'.

In an excellent paper on research methodology, Chess Denman (1995; herself an analyst as well as a researcher) listed the enormous difficulties involved in setting up effective studies into long-term therapy. These include the heterogeneity of the disorders treated, uncertainty about the natural history of each of these conditions (which of them is likely to improve spontaneously with time?), the inability to control extra-analytic, real-life events which can impact on the patient and alter his or her psychological status, the problem of establishing clear criteria for studies of outcome, variations in style and therapeutic procedures between different institutes and schools of analysis, and so on, to say nothing of the huge costs which any long-term study must incur.

One way of reducing the cost factor has been developed by Wolfram Keller and his colleagues of the Free University of Berlin, who approached 111 former patients, who had received long-term Jungian analysis (i.e., more than 100 sessions), six years after their treatment was completed. Objective estimates of improvement or deterioration were provided by health insurance claims made by the subjects five years before and five years after their analysis. As many as 94 per cent of the subjects reported substantial and lasting improvement in their mental state, their general satisfaction with life, their performance at work and their personal relationships. This corresponded with assessments independently provided by their former therapists and also with a reduction in the number of days spent off work for sickness or for treatment in hospital, as well as the number of out-patient visits to a doctor and prescriptions received for drugs. Since these strongly positive findings are at variance with those derived from other long-term outcome studies, they will require confirmation from other sources.

A major difficulty confronted by those organizing such studies is the fact that many analysts remain consistently hostile to the entire notion of research into what they do. They argue that the procedures involved (taping sessions, interviewing patients during treatment, etc.) would interfere with the therapeutic process, and that research focusing on symptom-removal and other behavioural measures completely overlooks the very stuff of analysis which is concerned with the inner life of the patient. Moreover, their entrenched scepticism of research means that, when findings conflict with their theories, these analysts invariably question the research methodology rather than the value of the theory.

They argue that the studies so far completed have been conducted on poorly selected patients who may not always have been appropriate for psychoanalytic treatment, and that the practitioners providing the treatment were usually trainees rather than experienced analysts. But, as Chess Denman shrewdly observed, there are limits to the length of time that a form of treatment can claim to be considered 'promising' but 'insufficiently researched'. Psychoanalysts have had over 100 years to prove what they do is more valuable than other approaches and so far they have conspicuously failed to do so.

It is precisely because funding decisions are based increasingly on outcome studies and 'clinical audits' that it is unlikely that government agencies or insurance companies will be willing to finance psychoanalytic treatment in the future and that this expensive, long-term treatment may be confined to patients who are rich, undiscriminating and not particularly ill. Psychoanalysts have always claimed that their form of intensive therapy is indispensable to bringing about any radical improvement in people with deep-seated personality disorders. But, here again, the evidence is against them. Such disorders are extremely difficult to treat by whatever methods have been tried, and psychoanalysis has no greater success to its credit than any other therapeutic approach. If anything, it has been shown to be less effective than cognitive behaviour therapy in this regard. So, what is left? Should psychoanalysis see itself no longer as a means of treatment for psychiatric disorders and more as a mode of cultural education designed to enrich the personality and enhance the quality of life of those who have the time and money to devote to it? Even allowing for the modifications post-Freudians have made to Freud's basic tenets, this is perhaps the more honest position for psychoanalysts to adopt—at least with psychoanalysis in its present form, with its present postulates and procedures.

In the absence of clear evidence that psychoanalysis is indeed more effective in the treatment of neurotic and personality disorders than briefer, less expensive forms of treatment, it should relinquish its claims to be a superior 'treatment of choice' for these conditions. Rather it should accept that what therapeutic achievements it can claim are based on principles common to all other forms of psychotherapy and be clear about what it is, if anything, that psychoanalysis may add to them. Otherwise, it will disappear, like so many other mythologies, into the mists of history.

The active ingredients

What, then, has research demonstrated the active ingredients of psychotherapy to be? From their extensive reviews of such research, David Orlinsky of Chicago University and his colleagues (2004) were able to define definite links between the processes involved in psychotherapy and their positive outcome for patients. Overwhelmingly, this research pointed to the crucial importance of the therapeutic bond or alliance. It is essential that this alliance should be experienced as positive and supportive and that it should be based on a 'collaborative sharing of responsibility', as both participants focus on the patient's feelings, experiences and difficulties. It is also important that the therapist should be perceived as skilful as well as sympathetic and that the patient should be open, non-defensive and actively committed to the therapeutic process. There is also some evidence that longer treatment duration (rather than greater number of sessions) is associated with a more lasting positive outcome, but this has to be confirmed.

Essentially, these are the factors advocated by Jung in the treatment of patients in analysis, and they are affirmed by many other studies. Again and again, patients report the most valued aspects of therapy to be a warm, positive relationship with a likeable therapist (e.g., Conte et al., 1995), and therapists who are rated as unhelpful are those felt to be cold, impersonal and lacking in compassion (e.g., Glass and Arnkoff, 2000).

All these factors apply to the practice of psychoanalysis as well as to other therapies. What psychoanalysis would claim to add to them specifically are the transference and its interpretation. Is there evidence to support the psychoanalytic contention that this procedure is crucial for long-term success? In order to answer this William Henry (1994) of Vanderbilt University and his colleagues undertook a detailed review of empirical studies of transference interpretations and their outcome. They concluded that far from contributing to positive therapeutic results, 'several studies have linked greater frequency of transference interpretations to poorer outcomes'. What is more, 'transference interpretations do not necessarily repair poor alliances and may damage the existing alliance'. Transference interpretations do not deepen the intensity of the analytic experience in comparison with non-transference interventions, and they are 'more likely to elicit defensive responding than any other types of interventions'.

Similarly, other researchers have found that higher frequencies of transference interpretation are associated with poorer outcomes (e.g. Hogland, 1993) and with higher rates of drop-out (Piper et al., 1999).

Since there is universal agreement that the decisive factor for positive outcome in psychotherapy is, as Jung maintained, the establishment of a good, close working alliance between the patient and the therapist, it would seem that, on the basis of William Henry's and Hans Strupp's findings, the emphasis placed on transference analysis by Freudian, Kleinian and Fordhamite Jungians adds little to what is provided by other schools of psychotherapy and, indeed, may be anti-therapeutic.

Transference interpretations can be experienced as helpful, however, provided that they are made sparingly, that the patient acknowledges them to be accurate, that they are made within the context of a positive therapeutic alliance, and are expressed in such a way as not to devalue the actual non-transference relationship (Piper et al., 1999).

One early research finding that rather upset the counselling and therapeutic professions was that clients who sought help from paraprofessional non-qualified practitioners were more likely to report favourable outcomes than those who consulted professionals. (e.g., Durlak, 1979; Hattie et al., 1984). It seems that some people are naturally gifted psychotherapists, whether qualified or not. As Mick Cooper observes: 'The key therapist factors are not so much to do with *who* therapists are, but *how* they relate to their clients.'

But what all these forms of research fail to reveal is the quality of the exchanges that occur in the analytic session—the way in which the significant meanings that dominate a patient's life are recovered, experienced, formulated and 'reconstructed'—and what this means in terms of the patient's aesthetic of living. Here it may be that the intensive dialectic of the analytic situation has the edge on other forms of therapy, but, again, the quality of both analyst and patient as people as well as the richness of their exchanges will be decisive. Such factors, however, are difficult—if not impossible—to measure. It is at this point that the line between science and art grows hazy, and where therapy becomes more a matter of culture and philosophy than of scientific empiricism.

What is clear is that the old certainties are crumbling. The iron curtain separating the Freudians from the Kleinians and the great wall separating both from the Jungians are beginning to disintegrate. But as Thomas Kuhn (1962) has shown, old paradigms do not yield directly to scientific disproof but only to a new, more attractive paradigm when it emerges to take its place.

It is possible that this new paradigm is already upon us, and it is time that we examined its characteristics to determine what it may have to offer.

3
EVOLUTIONARY PSYCHOTHERAPY:
THE NEW PARADIGM

A central concern for all schools of psychotherapy is the question: what has gone wrong for the patient in the first place? The major schools have come up with different answers to the same question, and different solutions as to how the problem may be put right. To the classical Freudian the problem is the repressed urges and memories of childhood which need to be made conscious; to the object relations theorist it is the formation of a false self at the expense of the real self which the analytic relationship must undo and correct; to the attachment theorist it is the pathological development of an internal working model of the self as incapable of receiving and giving love that needs to be readjusted; to the Jungian it is the frustrated archetypal intent which needs to be liberated so that the patient can achieve his or her full potential; to the microbiological psychiatrist it is the absence or excessive presence of some biochemical substance which needs to be corrected; while to the clinical psychiatrist it is the presence of some pathological process or disease which needs to be diagnosed and treated with pills or electric shocks. What, if anything, can the evolutionary perspective add to this already crowded playground of aetiological and therapeutic ideas?

The solution evolutionary psychiatry proposes is both elegantly simple and compatible with Jungian theory. Through the process of natural selection, specific patterns of behaviour emerged which effectively solved the problems of survival during the hunter-gatherer stage of human development. These patterns, or archetypes, became encoded in our genetic make-up, and they continue to affect how people behave in contemporary situations.

Far from being a blank slate, the human mind possesses a large repertoire of genetically encoded psychological mechanisms that enable us to respond adaptively to the social and physical eventualities that the environment creates from moment to moment. How, then, do psychiatric disorders arise?

Evolutionary psychiatry takes the view that the symptoms that cause people to seek treatment—depression, anxiety, phobias, mania, delusions, hallucinations, obsessive-compulsive phenomena, etc.—are not signs of 'disease' but natural responses with which all members of our species are equipped. These responses become troublesome in certain people when they are exaggerated or distorted, occur in inappropriate situations, or result from genetic biases. According to this view, the development of a child into an adult may be broadly compared to the development of an acorn. The acorn will become the best oak tree it can, given the kind of soil, the condition of the climate, the proximity and height of the surrounding trees, and so on. Deficiencies in any of these environmental conditions will result in stunting or distorted growth.

The meaning of anxiety and depression

A great advantage of looking at psychiatric symptoms from an evolutionary standpoint is that it renders them *meaningful*. That mental symptoms could have a biological basis is not a new idea. In his essay, 'A Phylogenetic Fantasy', Freud suggested that certain states of mind, such as paranoia and anxiety, were remnants of responses which were biologically adaptive in human beings up to the time of the Ice Age. Jung also believed that such states possessed an evolutionary basis which predated the family conflicts that figure so extensively in the psychoanalytic literature.

Unfortunately, by insisting that anxiety is a classifiable 'illness', psychiatrists have given the impression that anxiety is a 'neurotic' condition that no well-adjusted person should ever experience. Viewed in the evolutionary perspective, however, the capacity to experience anxiety is *indispensable* to survival, for an animal incapable of fear is a dead animal. The dodo died because it had always inhabited an environment without predators and knew no fear. But when humans arrived, bringing predators with them, this tame and fearless creature rapidly succumbed to them and became extinct.

In clinical practice, psychiatrists distinguish between patients who suffer from 'free-floating anxiety' (which can be triggered by anything and everything) and those who suffer from 'phobic anxiety' (which is triggered by specific objects or situations). However, the actual physical, emotional and psychological components of anxiety, fear and panic are broadly similar whatever the triggering factor may be, and their biological function is to promote survival by facilitating an appropriate response—whether this be violence, escape, submission, or 'freezing'. Thus, predators promote flight, weak challengers promote attack, strong challengers stimulate submission, and high places cause freezing. Specific phobic anxieties are thus often linked to specific forms of response. Fear of heights (acrophobia) promotes *freezing* rather than escape, because it renders one less likely to fall; fear of blood (haemophobia) causes *fainting* with its associated slowing of the heart rate and lowering of blood pressure (thus rendering one less likely to bleed to death). Fear of open or public spaces (agoraphobia) causes one to stay at home (thus rendering one less likely to be mugged or raped), while fear of flying (aerophobia) keeps one on the ground (thus making it impossible to be killed in an air crash).

Naturally enough, these links are not always specific. After all, fear of spiders, fear of snakes (and fear of animals in general) results in avoidance, freezing, escape or attack according to one's appraisal of the situation. When it comes to responding to anxiety, it is one's appraisal of precisely what is happening that is the crucial factor. To misquote Kipling, 'If you can keep your head when all about you are losing theirs, it's just possible that you haven't grasped the situation!'

To be seized by an attack of phobic anxiety is to experience the power of what Jung called 'an autonomous complex' operating at an ancient and unconscious level of the brain. You may realize how absurdly irrational it is to be terrified of a little spider in the bath, but your higher, recently evolved, cerebral capacities are incapable of doing anything to control it. You have to withdraw and leave somebody else to deal with the spider.

This, as it happens, is the usual way of coping with a phobia: one does everything possible to avoid proximity to the source of the fear. Being quite unable to control it, one has no option but to keep away from everything associated with it. This is the biological 'purpose' of the fear concerned. It is 'designed' to keep one out of harm's way. That is why it evolved, and why it has remained as part of our behavioural repertoire.

Evidently, situations are assessed at different levels of the brain, and conflicts can arise between these levels as to what strategy one should adopt. At the conscious level, you may tell yourself not to be silly, that it's only a harmless little spider, and that you should swat it with the loofah and stop making a fuss. Instead, you find yourself running out of the bathroom, screaming for help. Clearly, you have been taken over by a defensive response, which is beyond voluntary control because it is located beyond the reach of consciousness in a part of the old mammalian brain (which is incorporated within the human brain) known as the limbic system.

Anxiety disorders are of considerable interest, therefore, because they provide an example of an archetype entering the personal psyche as a complex. When the various phobias suffered by modern men and women are examined in detail, there is, in fact, little that is modern about them. They are all exaggerated fears of objects, animals or situations that were potentially life threatening in the environment in which our species evolved and in which we are adapted to live. This vital point is invariably overlooked in textbooks of psychiatry and it represents a key insight of the evolutionary approach to human psychopathology.

Anxiety and fear are adaptive responses to the kinds of dangers humans have been exposed to in the course of their evolution. This is why we fear ancient dangers such as snakes, spiders, high or open places, and not modern dangers such as cars, cigarettes, whisky and saturated fats, which kill off our contemporaries in infinitely greater numbers. Modern phobias, such as of going to school, going out to do the shopping, going to the dentist, or contracting AIDS, are contemporary versions of adaptive fears of going off the home range, getting hurt or becoming diseased. Some modern phobias are composites of ancestral fears: for example, fear of flying is made up of biologically appropriate fears of the primordial dangers represented by heights, falling, loud noise and being trapped in small, enclosed spaces from which there is no exit.

Another major group of psychiatric conditions, which is yielding to evolutionary insights, is made up of the affective or mood disorders, commonly known as manic-depression or bipolar disorder. That both depressive and manic reactions are adaptive is indicated by their universal occurrence throughout human communities in response to certain characteristic life events. The subjective sense of misery; the inability to take pleasure in anything; the complete loss of energy and drive; the feelings of anxiety, tension and worthlessness are *core* symptoms of depression that are recognized and diagnosed in different terminologies in all human societies throughout the world. It was my friend and colleague John Price who made the original observation that depression in human beings has features in common with the state that many different kinds of animals get into when they are defeated in conflicts for territory, mates or status within the rank hierarchy of their group. He realized that both mania and depression have an extremely long evolutionary history.

Three hundred million years ago our ancestors competed for resources, such as food, territory and mates, on an *individual* basis— as many vertebrates continue to do to this day. Then, as group living became established and territory began to be shared, individuals stopped competing directly for territory and instead began to compete for rank. Once acquired, high rank brought with it access to the resources that were desired.

Competition for rank took the form of threat displays and physical duels or tournaments. Very early on, animals evolved the capacity to assess their own strengths in comparison with an adversary and to make good guesses as to the probable outcome of being involved in a fight. On the basis of this guess, they attack, run away or submit.

This kind of behaviour is particularly apparent among reptiles, and the capacity for evaluating success or failure as well as the patterns of behaviour involved, must reside in the reptilian brain, vestiges of which persist in the oldest parts of our own brains.

Repeated successes in duels result in high self-assessment on the part of the animal, while defeats result in a lower self-assessment, which causes the animal to indulge in what behavioural biologists call the 'yielding subroutine'. What John Price recognized was that this defeated state, together with the proneness to make use of the 'yielding subroutine', provides the basis of the depressive reaction in human patients. The reason why the depressed state evolved, he argued, is because it provides a means of adapting to loss—whether it be loss of rank, or loss of a loved person. In other words, the adaptive function of the depression is to facilitate losing and to promote accommodation to the fact that one has lost. This has the effect of preventing the loser from suffering further injury and of preserving the stability and competitive efficiency of the group, which would otherwise be disrupted by constant battles for status and for sexual partners.

The typical life events that trigger either a depressive or a manic reaction, therefore, are the perception of one of two possible outcomes: loss or gain. What is lost or gained may be a spouse or a child, a job or financial security, health or reputation. But what the particular loss or gain amounts to in the long-term scale of ultimate biological objectives is a decrease or increase in the resources needed for reproductive success and getting one's genes into the next generation.

The evolutionary approach provides similar insights into such conditions as eating disorders, obsessive-compulsive phenomena and a variety of personality disorders. Readers wishing to follow up these leads will find them discussed in *Evolutionary Psychiatry: A New Beginning* (Second edition), which I wrote in collaboration with John Price and published in 2000.

Attachment, rank and psychopathology

The immediate cause of many psychiatric conditions may be understood as a subjective prediction on the part of the patient that he or she will fail in competing for two highly valued social resources: attachment and rank. We all need to feel that we are loved and worthy of love. We also need to feel that we have status in the eyes of others, because this determines the level of our self-esteem. If we feel unworthy of love and lacking in status, the result in especially vulnerable people is neurosis or psychosis or any one of a number of personality disorders.

Interest in the evolutionary history of competitiveness for rank and resources has, understandably, proved controversial. The commitment of social scientists to ideas of cultural relativity and behavioural plasticity (together with a tendency to idealise the apparently egalitarian spirit of surviving hunter-gatherer communities) has meant that the importance universally attributed to rank and status in human societies has been largely overlooked.

Recent acknowledgement of this oversight has resulted in the discovery that hunter-gatherer societies are in fact less egalitarian than they seemed. Not only is the propensity to form social hierarchies a universal and evolutionarily stable characteristic, but its phylogenetic antiquity may be deduced from ethological studies of our closest relatives—the chimpanzees, the bonobos (pygmy chimpanzees) and the gorillas—among whom hierarchies of varying degrees of complexity are indispensable to their social organization. That the phylogenetic history of human social competitiveness has come to assume special interest for evolutionary psychiatrists is because it appears to be deeply implicated in the psychopathology of such a large number of psychiatric disorders.

Two major archetypal systems

Some time in the last ten million years a new form of social competition has arisen: instead of trying to intimidate rivals, a competitor seeks to attract them. This form of competition is apparent, for example, among chimpanzees, and its significance was first recognized by the primatologist Michael Chance. In addition to threat displays, male chimpanzees indulge in a form of behaviour that is not threatening at all and does not demand the submission of a subordinate. Rather it is a form of social solicitation, which, Chance noted, results in affiliative behaviour 'in which there is a continuing interaction between individuals, such as grooming, play, sexual or mothering behaviour with the displayer' (Chance and Jolly, 1970).

In the course of extensive observations on social groups of primates, Chance recognized that they had two quite distinct modes of functioning, which he termed *agonic* and *hedonic*. The agonic mode is characteristic of hierarchically organized societies where individuals are concerned with warding off threats to their status and inhibiting overt expressions of aggressive conflict; while the hedonic mode is associated with affiliative behaviour in more egalitarian social organizations where agonic tensions are absent.

While acknowledging the pitfalls involved in translating animal findings to human social psychology, many researchers have come to see Chance's two modes as possessing great explanatory value. Numerous parallels exist in the history of ideas: for example, Empedocles' distinction between love and strife (from which Freud derived his Eros and Thanatos instincts), Aristotle's distinction between the political and hedonic life, and the classical sociological distinction made by the German social theorist Ferdinand Tonnies (1855–1936), between *Gemeinschaft* and *Gesellschaft*. In short, there is good reason to propose the existence of *two major archetypal systems:*

(1) *hedonic*—that concerned with attachment, affiliation, care-giving, care-receiving and altruism

(2) *agonic*—that concerned with rank, status, discipline, law and order, territory and possessions.

These may well be the basic archetypal patterns on which social adjustment and maladjustment, psychiatric health and sickness depend. Both can function healthily when evoked in appropriate circumstances; but either can give rise to pathology when their goals are frustrated or when they are inappropriately activated.

It was the evolutionary replacement of intimidation by attraction that allowed the hedonic mode to emerge. In the hedonic mode, competitors seek to disarm potential rivals, attract potential mates and achieve status in the eyes of other members of the group.

Group approbation of competitors' displays has the effect of raising their self-esteem. Should their displays be met with disapprobation, on the other hand, individuals become less attractive to potential mates, lose status in the eyes of the group and suffer a reduction in self-esteem.

Thus, attractive people are granted prestige. They tend to assume leadership roles and have access to more resources than their less successful competitors. In environments similar to the environment in which we evolved (the so-called 'ancestral environment') they tend, as with the Ache of Paraguay and the !Kung Bushmen of the Kalahari, to have more wives, sire more children, and their children are more likely to survive. Their 'fitness', in biological terms, therefore increases.

Psychopathology explained

Essentially, the possible outcomes of competition through dominance and attraction can be represented diagrammatically, as shown in Figure 1, with physical competition for dominance on a vertical axis, and competition by attraction for approval and social integration on a horizontal axis.

The horizontal dimension may also be labelled approach–withdrawal, closeness–distance, friendliness–hostility, in-group–out-group orientation, love–hate, etc. In other words, the horizontal

79

dimension is concerned with affiliation, while the vertical dimension is concerned with power. The horizontal needs, of course, resemble Jung's 'extraversion–introversion' dimension in his theory of psychological types.

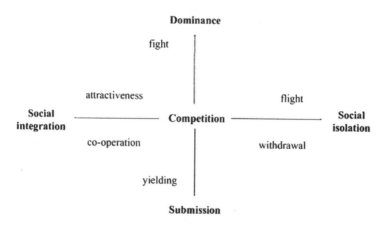

Figure 1. A schema for possible outcomes of competition through dominance and attraction

The broad application of these basic dimensions to human psychopathology results in the following indications:

Successful affiliation is associated with social adjustment and mental health.

Failure in affiliation is associated with an introverted, inner-directed mode of personality adjustment that may give rise to personality disorders of the schizoid, schizotypal or paranoid type, or result in a schizophrenic breakdown.

Submission is associated with low self-esteem, feelings of shame and humiliation, anxiety, depression, masochism, dependent personality disorder and a liability to be victimized or abused.

Dominance is associated with high self-esteem, hypomania, sadism and a liability to abuse others.

80

Insiders and outsiders

The crucial factor determining the kind of disorder individuals will present is whether or not they continue to feel themselves to be 'insiders' (i.e., members of the in-group, committed to membership of the community, whether loved or unloved, of high status or low) or 'outsiders' (i.e., not members of the in-group, not committed to membership of the community, not involved in attachment relationships or in conflicts for status). If an 'insider' develops a psychiatric disorder, it will tend to be a *disorder of attachment and rank* (e.g., anxiety disorder, affective disorder, obsessive-compulsive disorder, etc.), whereas an 'outsider' will tend to develop a *spacing disorder* (e.g., schizoid personality disorder or schizophrenia).

Individuals who are uncertain as to their allegiance and who hover uneasily on the cusp between 'insider' and 'outsider' status will, if they develop a psychiatric disorder, tend to present with a *borderline* state (e.g., borderline or schizotypal personality disorder). See Figure 2.

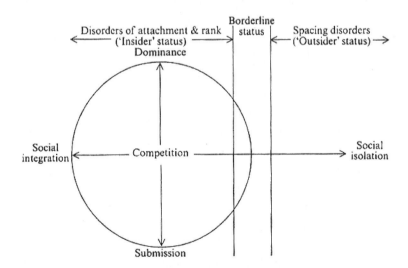

Figure 2. A schema for the classification of the major disorders

The beauty of this new classificatory schema is that it helps to move us beyond the old 'medical model', with its emphasis on the diagnosis and treatment of dubious 'mental diseases', towards an entirely new conceptual framework that defines the basic components of human nature in terms of their evolutionary origins and their essential developmental needs.

This new paradigm does not contradict those earlier psychiatric or psychoanalytic findings and formulations, which are empirically valid, but enables them to be incorporated within a more embracing and ultimately more satisfactory explanatory system. It permits the statement of a basic principle of psychopathology that may be summed up as follows:

> *Psychopathology results when the environment fails, either partially or totally, to meet one (or more) archetypal need(s) in the developing individual* or, in Jungian terms, *when the environment is responsible for the frustration of archetypal intent.*

This is John Bowlby's postulate, with his added corollary that the *further the rearing environment deviates from the environment of evolutionary adaptedness* (i.e., the ancestral environment) the *greater is the likelihood of pathological development.* If we are to understand the psychiatric disorders from which our contemporaries suffer, then we have to take into account the ways (as Jung did in *Modern Man in Search of a Soul)* in which Western society frustrates the needs of the Palaeolithic man or woman still persisting as living potential within us in our present environmental circumstances.

Many possibilities come to mind: the disruption of community-based kinship bonds as a result of migration, job mobility, experiments in town planning, and so on; the disruption of families through divorce and separation, together with the rapidly increasing incidence of single-parent families; the loss of female support groups of the kind provided by traditional communities; the lack of adequate provision for the secure and intimate care of children whose mothers go out to work; the occurrence of negative life events, such as losing one's job, being passed over for promotion, mortgage rate increases, house repossessions, exam or interview failures, difficulty in acquiring the necessary skills demanded by employers, and sedentary work in artificial light and controlled atmospheres; the loss of myth, ritual and religion; the lack of contact with nature, the seasons and the primordial environment.

All these factors are potentially productive of stress, insecurity and 'anomie' as well as distorted development. It is not unlikely that the various neuroses, psychopathies, drug dependencies, the occurrence of child and spouse abuse, to say nothing of the alarming crime statistics, are connected with Western society's inability to satisfy the archetypal needs of our kind. Many of these points were impressively emphasized by Glantz and Pearce in their book *Exiles From Eden: Psychotherapy from an Evolutionary Perspective* (1989).

A key factor in the causation of most psychiatric illness is *stress*. The probability is that the greater the gap between archetypal needs and environmental fulfilment of those needs, the greater the stress and the more incapacitating the subsequent disorder.

Kinship libido and the therapeutic alliance

Although many people suffering from stress come to the attention of psychiatrists, a large number of them, perhaps the majority, do not; nor do they necessarily manifest the signs of psychiatric illness. As early as the 1930s Jung was reporting that a good two-thirds of the patients who consulted him were not suffering from a diagnosable psychiatric disorder but from the meaninglessness and purposelessness of their lives. The same is true of the majority of people who consult psychotherapists at the present time.

What, then, has the evolutionary paradigm to offer the practising psychotherapist?

The answer is that it can revolutionize the old psychoanalytic model for psychotherapy in the same way as it may replace the old medical model for psychiatry and, as a result, inaugurate a more effective as well as a more optimistic therapeutic philosophy.

Freud needed to believe in resistance and in an unconscious that was atavistic, disorganized and chaotic so that he could continue to believe in his theories and impose them on his patients. By contrast, evolutionary psychotherapy views the programs operative in the unconscious as essentially adaptive, organized and directed towards specific goals. It sees the patient as the primary agent of change, and seeks to activate the innate psychological mechanisms (or 'algorithms') responsible for hedonic social interaction, so as to provide support, insight and understanding along 'kinship' lines.

Moreover, Neo-Darwinian theory has thus given a new meaning to Jung's concept of 'kinship libido' and has added a whole new dimension to both the transference and the therapeutic alliance. Darwin believed that success in the struggle for survival, linked with success in competing for the attraction of sexual partners, enhanced an individual's *reproductive fitness*—that is, it increased the number of copies of his or her genetic material that the individual passed on to *direct* descendants.

However, the classical Darwinian view of sexual reproductive fitness focused on the *individual* and this has proved inadequate to explain certain elements of behaviour, such as self-sacrifice and altruism. As a result, it has been found necessary to replace the Darwinian notion of reproductive fitness with the Neo-Darwinian concept of *inclusive* fitness.

In the contemporary evolutionary view, what matters more than the survival of the individual *per se* is the survival of that individual's genes. Inclusive fitness refers to the number of copies of their genetic material that individuals cause to be passed on, not only to their direct descendants, but to *other* than direct descendants as well—for example, to nephews, nieces and cousins, all of whom share a proportion of their genes.

This has given rise to a variety of what are termed 'response rules', 'strategies' and 'tactics' for the performance of social behaviours that promote the probability of gene survival—for example, the care and protection of children, peer bonding and peer play, status-seeking, competing for valued resources, courtship, sexual bonding and marriage, sharing and storing food, seeking shelter, co-operating, reciprocal altruism, discriminating against strangers, the splitting of groups when they achieve a critical size, the expression of out-group hostility and in-group loyalty, cleaning, washing, grooming, teaching, ritualized tournaments, subscribing to the beliefs and practices of myth, religion and ritual, and so on.

In the ancestral environment human beings lived in small groups in which some genetic relationship existed between all members. As a result, these strategies were usually directed towards kin or shared with kin, while wariness and hostility were reserved for strangers. *It is within this kin-oriented matrix that the therapeutic relationship needs to operate if it is to stand any chance of success.*

The positive orientation towards kin—to help, support and succour them—so apparent in human communities throughout the world, has both 'ultimate' and 'proximate' functions:

The *ultimate function* is to get one's genes into the next generation. Genetic 'fitness' is a relative concept: your fitness is greater than your neighbour's, if more of your genes appear in the next generation. The genetic arithmetic of individual fitness is straightforward: parents share 50 per cent of their genes with each offspring and 25 per cent with each grandchild. If you have a nephew, he will share, on average, 25 per cent of your genes. One of his offspring will have 12.5 per cent of your genes. Therefore, if he has five offspring, a greater number of your genes will be replaced in the next generation than if you had only one son (12.5 per cent × 5 = 62.5 per cent, as opposed to 50 per cent) In practice, this gives rise to trade-offs that influence behaviour in predictable ways. Thus, parents tend to invest more in their offspring than in less genetically close relatives, and children who live with one natural and with one step-parent are more likely to be abused than children living with two natural parents.

The *proximate consequences* of this strategy of kin preference not only influence our behaviour to parents, siblings, offspring, nephews and nieces, but also to people experienced and related to 'as if' they were kin. Psychological kinship thus extends further than biological kinship, and this is probably explained by the fact that we evolved to live in small communities where the majority of the members were kin. Indeed, the propensity to distinguish kin from non-kin could underlie all in-group/out-group dichotomies.

Accordingly, kinship theory offers a deeper understanding of Bowlby's attachment concept. As the evolutionary psychologist Mark Erickson (2000) has shown, early secure attachment to immediate kin mobilizes adaptive kin-directed behaviours in later life, such as preferential altruism and incest avoidance. Impaired attachment early in life predicts aberrant kin-directed behaviour including diminished altruism, as well as neglect and an increased incidence of incest.

Thus, attachment may be conceived as the primary developmental function of both the psychological experience of kinship and of the adaptive kinship behaviour that goes with it. As Erickson says, this points to an innate psychology of kinship that has evolutionary roots far more ancient than our own species. And it would seem highly probable that constellation of 'psychological kinship' within the analytic relationship is one of the most crucial factors contributing to successful outcome.

Evolutionary implications for treatment

In addition to indicating the importance of being unconsciously classified as 'kin', the evolutionary paradigm provides further guidance for the psychotherapist. Since patients are almost invariably suffering from feelings of insecurity, connected with low self-esteem and doubts about their love-worthiness, it follows that the therapist should carry out John Bowlby's prescription to provide an accepting and welcoming environment, so that the consulting room is experienced as a safe haven or 'secure base'. The therapist's attitude should essentially be one of 'care-giving' and should offer social attention and approval in such a way as to enhance the patient's sense of personal status and self-esteem. Only when these basic parameters have been established should the therapist begin to provide insight into internal models that are evidently proving dysfunctional in the life of the patient.

One defect of much psychotherapy research is that it does not take adequate account of the possibility that people with different problems may respond better to different kinds of treatment. As a result, patients with phobias, obsessions, depression, feelings of inadequacy, marital problems and different kinds of personality disorder have, in many studies, all been lumped together and given the same kind of therapy. From the scientific standpoint, this is about as sophisticated as studying the results of administering aspirin to a group of patients with a large number of different medical disorders. As Paul Gilbert (2000) has observed, psychotherapists should not be expected to be one-club golfers: they should be equipped with a number of different clubs appropriate to the task in hand. The advantage of the evolutionary approach is that it studies each patient to discover what is the specific archetypal issue at the heart of the problem. Once that has been determined, it becomes possible to suggest what therapeutic measure is most likely to be helpful.

For people suffering from clearly established psychiatric disorders, therefore, the evolutionary perspective provides useful therapeutic indicators, as, for example, in the treatment of phobic anxiety or depression. Phobic patients usually feel ashamed of their symptoms, believing that they are the only people in the world to be so afflicted, and that their irrational fears represent some dreadful pathological weakness in their character. The treatment offered by conventional psychiatry usually does little to alleviate this profoundly negative self-perception. When, however, such patients learn that what they are suffering is not some sick, personal aberration but a response shared with all humanity as an innate defence mechanism, it comes as a reassurance and a great relief.

Similarly, agoraphobia can be understood as an innate fear of straying from the home base. Most animals are territorial. Once they have established a territory, they defend it vigorously against all comers and are usually victorious. Some species have a home range that they patrol and share with other members of their species. But few seem happy to leave their home range, and it is the ability to leave home without anxiety that is exceptional and which requires explanation.

When treating such patients, it is helpful to bear in mind the association that exists in the majority of animal species between territorial ownership and the display of self-confidence and self-esteem. A rise in self-esteem can increase the home range of agoraphobic patients: it is as if they feel they have a right to patrol a larger area, and, as a result, their sense of being an intruder when they stray off their home ground is reduced. Research has established that a rise in self-esteem lowers both subjective anxiety and physiological arousal. Thus, to boost the self-esteem of agoraphobic patients may be a more effective remedy than attempting to 'decondition' their anxiety by taking them into those places which they most fear—an heroic therapy that often works but can result in a reinforcement of their conditioned aversion.

Another therapeutic measure that can prove effective with agoraphobics is to encourage good relations with neighbours, so as to transform alien territory (which patients unconsciously anticipate to be agonistically defended) into a home range (which can be hedonically shared). One large group of agoraphobic patients consists of women who do not go out to work. It is helpful for these patients to be reassured that there is nothing absurd about preferring to remain safely at home instead of going out shopping on their own. After all, there were no supermarkets in the ancestral environment, and 'gathering' was almost certainly done in the reassuring intimacy of familiar groups of women.

Similarly, when confronted with a depressed patient, a therapist who appreciates the evolutionary meaning of depressive reactions will take care to form a clear understanding of what precisely it is that the patient has lost and has, perforce, to give up. As long as the patient refuses to accept the loss, and remains committed to a hopeless desire to recover what has been lost, he or she will remain depressed. When the loss has been truly acknowledge and accepted, is it likely that the depression will lift.

The new synthesis

By far the most important function that the evolutionary approach can perform is a grand, all-embracing work of synthesis and integration. By providing a new scientific paradigm within which fundamental questions about human nature can be formed and answered, it can bring together the disparate findings of ethology, sociology, psychology and cross-cultural anthropology within one theoretical perspective—the Darwinian perspective, which promises to become the central conceptual standpoint uniting all behavioural sciences.

This trend has now moved so far that it is unlikely that any psychological explanation will stand much chance of surviving in the future if it is incompatible with the Darwinian evolutionary consensus. This wider vision, by allowing us to see beyond the old medical and psychoanalytic models, must have an impact on all psychiatric and psychotherapeutic research and practice. It could succeed in reconciling the differences between 'biological', 'clinical' and 'social' psychiatry and could render obsolete the doctrinal squabbles and internecine battles between the classical schools of analysis.

This work was well begun as the last century was drawing to a close. For example, there was the publication of a special issue of the *British Journal of Medical Psychology* on evolutionary psychotherapy, published in September 1998; and *Genes on the Couch: Explorations in Evolutionary Psychotherapy*, edited by Paul Gilbert and Kent Bailey, published in 2000. The advance has been sustained into the present century, much of it under the creative influence of such workers as Paul Gilbert (2009; 2010), Jay Belsky (2007), Jerome Bolhuis (2011) and Dennis Tirch (2012) to name

89

but a few.

By transcending the old differences, however, it does not follow that the knowledge and insights gained during the past century of psychiatric and analytic practice must be lost or negated; rather, they will be absorbed within a more inclusive corpus of scientific understanding. Already, evolutionary psychotherapy has greatly extended the heuristic and empirical implications of archetypal theory, conceiving archetypes as 'innate algorithms' responsible for processing emotional, non-verbal information at a largely unconscious level of experience in accordance with certain specific 'biosocial goals'.

In common with object relations and attachment theorists, evolutionary psychologists share the view that human beings are, by nature, extraordinarily sensitive to social relationships, whether these be positive (e.g., love, attachment, friendship, sex: relationship in the hedonic mode) or negative (e.g., jealousy, guilt, shame, anxiety, depression, anger: relationship in the agonic mode). But since evolutionary psychology places equal emphasis on psychological and physical events, it permits research findings from psychology, biochemistry and neuroscience to be integrated with those of analysis and psychiatry. The elated sense of being loved and appreciated, for example, is associated with high blood levels of 5-HT (hydroxytryptamine) and with low levels of stress hormones, whereas the depressed feeling of being unloved and rejected is associated with low levels of 5-HT and high levels of stress hormones.

That the inherent strategies underlying these social experiences with their associated physiological mechanisms are evolutionarily ancient is evident from the fact that they are present in many species of animal that evolved long before *Homo sapiens sapiens*. As Paul Gilbert (personal communication) has pointed out:

> We now know that the brain comes with a range of basic motivational systems such as seeking to form attachments with caregivers. But what we also know is that the social experiences of the in-

fant, child and later adult are constantly changing the infrastructure of the brain in subtle ways. For example child-rearing practices can even impact on genetic expression (Belsky et al., 2011) and it is well known now that because of neurplasticity change in the brain is happening all the time. So the Darwinian approach is not only to understand the innate dispositions that we are born with, but also how they are shaped into phenotypes (the actual characteristics of the developing individual) from the beginnings of life in the womb and on through life. The basic research now is to explore the nature and potential variation in phenotypes, and the implications for psychotherapy.

How would Jung have reacted to these developments? I believe he would have been both fascinated and delighted. 'Man "possesses" many things which he has never acquired but has inherited from his ancestors.', Jung wrote,

He is not born as a tabula rasa, he is merely born unconscious. But he brings with him systems that are organized and ready to function in a specifically human way, and these he owes to millions of years of human development. Just as the migratory and nest-building instincts of birds were never learnt or acquired individually, man brings with him at birth the ground-plan of his nature. These inherited systems correspond to the human situations that have existed since primeval times: youth and old age, birth and death, sons and daughters, fathers and mothers, mating, and so on. Only the individual consciousness experiences these things for the first time, but not the bodily system and the unconscious. (*CW* 4, para. 728).

What comes to be fixed in the genetic structure of a species is the predisposition to certain 'species-specific' forms of behaviour and experience. How has evolution brought this about? Darwin's answer was through natural selection. As a result of genetic mutations, which occur spontaneously and at random, an individual may acquire a characteristic or propensity that makes it better adapted than its fellows to respond appropriately to a certain typical situation, such as attack from a predator.

Being thus advantaged, this individual will tend to survive and

91

pass on its new genetic configuration to members of subsequent generations, who, possessing the desirable characteristic, will compete more effectively in the struggle for existence. As a result, the new attribute eventually becomes established as a standard component in the genetic structure of the species. It is in this manner that our archetypal propensities have become adapted to the typical situations encountered in human life. The repeated selection of fortuitous mutations, occurring through hundreds of thousands of generations and over millions of years, has resulted in the present genome of the human species. And the genome expresses itself as surely in the structure of the human psyche and in human patterns of behaviour as it does in the anatomy of the human physique.

Just as the ultimate biological 'purpose' of our existence is the perpetuation of our genes, so the transmission of our genes to the next generation is the ultimate cause of our behaviour. The archetypal propensities with which we are born are adapted to enable us to survive long enough in the environment in which we evolved to give our genes a fair chance of transmission to our offspring.

Biosocial goals and the main schools of analysis

A central issue on which the attention of evolutionary psychologists is focused is: 'What social problems have humans evolved ways of recognizing and solving?' So far there is general agreement that, as a species, we characteristically recognize and invest our resources in our own offspring, we endeavour to select 'good quality' mates, we recognize and relate to people who are likely to co-operate with rather than exploit us and, when it comes to conflict, we tend to challenge only those whom we stand a fair chance of defeating. These characteristics have been listed as 'biosocial goals': these include care-eliciting and care-giving (attachment behaviour); mate selection (sexual attraction, courtship, conception and mate retention); alliance formation (caring, co-operation, affiliation, aggression inhibition, friendship and reciprocal behaviour); and ranking behaviour (competition for resources, dominance and submissive behaviour, and gaining and maintaining status or rank).

From the standpoint of the historical overview that has formed the substance of all three volumes of this book, it is particularly striking that each of the biosocial goals detected by the evolutionary psychologists has in fact provided the primary area of concern for the major schools of analysis—namely, care-eliciting, care-giving and alliance formation (Klein, Winnicott, Bowlby); mate selection and sex (Freud); rank behaviour (Adler); and the whole concept of goal-directed behaviour subserved by the archetypal components of the Self—the very stuff of analytical psychology (Jung).

With the unifying perspective that evolutionary psychology offers, the empirical study of the basic programs running in the unconscious at last becomes a scientific possibility.

Dangers ahead

Although the evolutionary paradigm evidently has a great deal to be said for it, many people entertain serious reservations about applying Darwinian insights to human nature. They fear that psychology could degenerate into a form of biological fundamentalism, conceiving everything in terms of genetic determinants and encouraging a cold, ruthless scientific objectivity that would result in the denial of feeling, ethics, values and morality. Not only would this lead to immensely destructive kinds of psychotherapy, but it would also constitute a cultural disaster of incalculable proportions, compounded by the use of scientific procedures such as those designed to assess positive therapeutic outcome purely in terms of economic cost effectiveness. Many would argue that we have already moved too far in this direction, and that the attempt to systematise and regulate psychotherapeutic techniques in the form of 'manuals' is a frightening indication of what could be in store for us. I find myself much in sympathy with these arguments, and, while I am excited by the heuristic possibilities offered by the new paradigm, I would agree that we must be vigilant to protect ourselves from the dangers involved in embracing it.

The gravest threat could come from those fanatics, thrown up by every theoretical system, who believe they know what is best for humanity and who, placing themselves on the highest intellectual and moral ground, seek to impose these beliefs on everyone else, entirely 'for their own good'. Darwin would have been horrified by the thought that anyone could turn his discovery to such ends. To him it would have been inconceivable that scientists should use the facts of our biological nature to make rules about how we 'ought' to live our lives. Unlike Marxism, Darwinism is not a manifesto; and, unlike Freudianism, it is not a doctrine. Darwinism gives us profound insights into the facts of how our bodies, minds and typical behaviours evolved, but it can never dictate how we should live or how we should organize society. It can provide us with useful information about the nature of our innate psychic propensities and the sort of environmental circumstances they evolved to adapt us to, and this knowledge may help psychiatrists and psychotherapists to make more enlightened decisions than hitherto about how best to treat their patients: but evolutionary theory should never be applied further than that. The most crucial of our evolved capacities is consciousness, with its associated capacities to perceive meaning, to make ethical judgements and to override the basic programs that evolution has equipped us with. It is consciousness that provides us with our most precious asset —the freedom to choose.

Secondly, it is essential that psychology should not fall into the trap of promoting itself as a branch of sociobiology, embracing a simplistic view of human beings as mere fitness-maximizing genetic vehicles, for this obliterates the psychological level of analysis altogether. So much human experience and behaviour results from working out complex variations on sets of archetypal themes, and these just cannot be explained as expressions of the strategy of the genes.

Men, for example, do not look at erotic photographs in order to maximize their fitness, but because they are equipped with evolved psychological mechanisms that cause them to find images of nubile females sexually stimulating. By exciting themselves with erotic images, they are manipulating components of the psycho-sexual system (which, given the opportunity, *can* result in reproduction) purely for their own enjoyment. As Paul Gilbert has observed:

> what humans excel at is not only the type of competencies they possess, but the range of stimuli they can direct their mentalities to. For example, caring behaviour can be directed to other people, animals, plants (gardening), inanimate objects (one's car or house) and also oneself. And we gain pleasure from engaging in all of these ... It is this opening up of mentalities (like caring) to a wide field of things ... that may well have been important to human evolution. (Gilbert, 1998).

Moreover, archetypal systems exist in us as ever-present potential that may or may not be activated in our lifetime: a man may remain celibate, never get involved in a fight, never go hunting, or never go to war. A woman may never have a child. Though our genes are powerful influences, they do not turn us into unconscious automata. The social matrix in which we grow up, its rules, values, language, customs and ideals are mediating factors between our basic human nature and the kind of individual human being we become.

A compass and a new orientation

Our capacity for consciousness may have evolved to enable us to monitor environmental events in the interests of survival and reproductive success, but it also makes us aware of the meaning and quality of those events as they occur. In the words of St Augustine, we both exist and know that we exist, and rejoice in this existence and this knowledge. Evolutionary theory not only provides insights into the natural history of this extraordinary achievement, but at the same time grants a wide therapeutic perspective in which it is possible to relate peoples' sufferings to the totality of human experience, as it is now and always has been.

To those psychotherapists working within the Jungian tradition, the evolutionary approach is particularly appealing since it provides the phylogenetic basis of the collective unconscious. It amplifies the archetypal concept, extending it downwards into its biological roots and outwards into the realm of social behaviour. This is a necessary compensation for Jung's own contribution, constrained as it inevitably was by his psychological type and personal experience. Jung extended archetypal theory upwards into the spiritual realm and inwards into the realm of the introverted, symbolic life arising from the unconscious. The evolutionary perspective enables us to fill out the picture, furthering the enterprise which Jung began. It also reaffirms Jung's transpersonal view of the human situation. Instead of seeing personal problems as merely the product of familial and social circumstances, it examines them in the context of the evolved goals, needs and strategies that have determined human behaviour since our species came into existence on the African savannah.

From the evolutionary standpoint, a psychiatric disorder is not a medical disaster like cancer or a stroke but an ancient adaptive response that, for some contemporary reason, has become maladaptive to the detriment of the patient's emotional and social life. For like the Jungian, the evolutionary psychiatrist looks beyond the personal predicament and relates it to the story of humankind. Both appreciate that what has traditionally been classified as 'illness' is often a consequence of a potentially healthy organism struggling to meet the demands of life: symptom formation is itself an adaptive process. Both the Jungian and the evolutionary approaches are thus conducive to therapeutic optimism. Instead of forms of futile suffering, symptoms are seen as the growing pains of people struggling to adjust to the demands that life has put on them.

The evolutionary view also affirms Jung's insight that every human being is richly endowed with the archetypal potential of the species. This means that however disordered, one-sided, or constricted an individual's psychological development may be, the potential for further growth and better adaptation is nevertheless there, implicit in the psychophysical structure of the organism.

As a result, patients may be helped to grow beyond the defective or inadequate form of adjustment that their personal history has permitted.

This perhaps is the most important conceptual contribution that evolutionary psychotherapy has to make: it grants an expanded view of the self. The self is not just the sum total of one's personal life experiences, as the object relations theorists and self psychologists maintain, but the product of many millions of years of development. Within each one of us the vast potential of humanity is contained. This provides an added dimension to the individuation process of becoming as complete a human being as one's circumstances allow: *it is about integrating ontogeny with phylogeny*, uniting one's personal experience with the potential experience of humanity. It means making the most of the mentalities with which natural selection has equipped us and bringing them to fulfilment in our lives. Success in this endeavour will depend on the therapist's skill in releasing the unused creative potential in the patient's personality.

A model for this is provided by classical Jungian analysis, which seeks to mobilize archetypal components of the phylogenetic psyche by encouraging patients to dream, to fantasize, to paint, to open themselves to relationships with new friends, and to find new ways of relating to old ones, as well as becoming conscious of the strategies and conflicts that have been controlling their lives in the past. To make headway in such demanding work, therapists have to develop their own personality and creative abilities if they hope to do much more than patch up their patients and enable them to go on existing. As Jung observed, 'an analyst can help his patient just as far as he himself has gone and not a step further.' It is a heavy responsibility, but it makes the work of a committed therapist one of the most challenging and rewarding professions it is possible to embrace.

Whatever upheavals may be in store for us as a result of theoretical revisions, outcome studies, clinical audits and research on the biochemistry of the brain, the primary duty of the psychotherapist will remain the same: to put empathy, knowledge and professional skill at the service of the patient. To adopt an evolutionary approach is not to espouse a political cause, to submit to biological determinism, or to abandon a proper concern for ethical values. What such an approach does provide is a compass and a new orientation to steer us through the immense complexities of human psychology, its disorders and their treatment.

New psychotherapies continue to appear: new forms, new methods, new theories, new organizations—all offering new trainings, and most of them under-researched and under-evaluated. It is likely, as we have seen, that all successful psychotherapies are based on a small number of principles which have been known to be effective in bringing psychological relief and personal change for many generations. What is needed now is a corpus of informed knowledge about the relationships between individual experience, social influences and the phylogenetic propensities which guide and inform all human development. This is the program which Freud and Jung embarked upon at the beginning of the twentieth century. Now, as the new century progresses, carrying us into the future, we are, perhaps, in a better position to bring it to fruition.

GLOSSARY

Aetiology: that part of medical science that investigates the causes of disease.

Agonic mode: a mode of social interaction characteristic of hierarchically organized societies where individuals are concerned with warding off threats to their status and inhibiting overt expressions of aggressive conflict.

Algorithm: a genetically acquired learning mechanism that organizes experience into adaptive patterns specific to certain typical activities, such as mate selection, predator avoidance, site selection, and so on.

Amplification: a technique advocated by Jung for working with symbolical material (arising from dreams, fantasies, paintings, etc.). Whereas free association may reveal much about the personal context of a dream, amplification educes parallels from myth, literature, art, religion and anthropology to 'make ample' the symbolism involved and extend its range of meaning to the human condition as a whole.

Analytical psychologist: an analyst who subscribes to the theories and who practises the therapeutic techniques devised by Jung; to be distinguished from psychiatrist, psychoanalyst, psychologist and psychotherapist.

Ancestral environment: environment of evolutionary adaptedness; the environment in which our species evolved and in which it is adapted to live.

Anxious attachment: a term introduced by John Bowlby to describe the state of those who suffer from the fear that their attachment figures may either be lost or prove inaccessible.

Archetypes: a term introduced by Jung to denote innate neuropsychic centres possessing the capacity to initiate, control and mediate the common behavioural characteristics and typical experiences of all human beings irrespective of race, culture, creed or historical epoch. In the Jungian scheme of things, archetypes are the components of the collective unconscious.

Attachment: a tie of affection formed by one person or animal for another; in the sense used by Bowlby, the tie formed between an infant and its mother or mother-substitute.

Attachment behaviour: the characteristic forms of behaviour by which attachment bonds between individuals are expressed.

Basic trust: a term introduced by Erik Erikson for the conviction that a good maternal figure can engender in a child, through the development of a strong attachment bond, that it can trust her, the world and itself.

Behavioural systems: a term introduced by John Bowlby for goal-directed mechanisms operating cybernetically (like electronic systems, through positive and negative feedback) in both mother and child, which are responsible for attachment behaviour and for mediating the development and maintenance of attachment bonds.

Behaviourism: a theoretical approach to animal and human psychology that focuses on the objective study of actual behavioural responses while largely ignoring the existence of feelings or states of mind, since these are not public and not objectively verifiable.

Biosocial goals: the social goals for which we are biologically equipped to strive, such as care, protection, love and status.

Borderline personality: a concept applied to individuals whose personalities combine features of neurotic and psychotic symptomatology.

Charisma: a term derived from New Testament Greek meaning the gift of grace; introduced into sociology by Max Weber to describe an 'extraordinary quality' possessed by persons or objects, which is thought to give them unique and magical power.

Collective unconscious: a term introduced by C. G. Jung to designate those aspects of the psyche that are common to all humanity; synonymous with phylogenetic psyche.

Complex: a group or cluster of interconnected ideas and feelings that exert a dynamic effect on conscious experience and on behaviour. Complexes are to the ontogenetic psyche (or personal

100

unconscious) what archetypes are to the phylogenetic psyche (or collective unconscious), the one being dependent on the other in the sense that complexes are 'personations' of archetypes.

Countertransference: the analyst's transference onto the patient.

Delusion: a false belief; characteristic of psychosis.

Ego: the part of the personality which one consciously recognizes as 'I' or 'me'.

Environment of evolutionary adaptedness (EEA): see ancestral environment.

Epigenesis: a term derived from Greek (upon + genesis = generation); a biological theory of development proposed by C. H. Waddington (1957). It holds that the development of all biological characteristics, whether they be relatively sensitive or insensitive to environmental variation, is governed by the genome.

Epistemology: study of the basis of knowledge.

Ethology: the study of the behaviour of organisms living in their natural habitats.

Gene: the basic unit of heredity.

Genome: the complete genetic constitution of an organism; the entire genetic program characterizing the species.

Hallucination: a false sensory perception in the absence of external stimuli: characteristic of psychosis.

Hedonic mode: a mode of social interaction in which underlying dominance relations are not being challenged and agonic tensions are consequently absent, permitting individuals to be affiliative and to give their attention to recreational or task-oriented activities.

Hermeneutics: the art or discipline of interpretation.

Homeostasis: maintenance of balance between opposing mechanisms or systems.

Id: Latin for 'it'; used by Freud's translators for *'das Es'*. 'We approach the id with analogies: we call it a chaos, a cauldron full of seething excitations ... it is filled with energy reaching it from the instincts, but it has no organization, produces no collective will, but only a striving to bring about the satisfaction of instinctual needs subject to the observance of the pleasure-principle' (Freud, 1923).

Inclusive fitness: refers to the number of copies of an individual's genetic material that survive them, not only in direct descendants, but in other than direct descendants as well (e.g., nephews, nieces, cousins, brothers and sisters, all of whom share a proportion of his or her genes).

Individuation: a term used by C. G. Jung to designate the process of personality development which leads to the fullest possible actualization of the archetypal endowment of an individual: 'Individuation means becoming a single, homogeneous being, and, insofar as "individuality" embraces our innermost, last, and incomparable uniqueness, it also implies becoming one's own self. We could therefore translate individuation as "coming to selfhood" or "self-realization" ' (*CW* 7, para. 266).

Kin-selection: refers to the selection of genes that cause individuals to favour close kin on account of the high probability that they will share those genes. Strictly speaking 'kin' should include direct offspring (sons and daughters), but many biologists have come to apply the term 'kin-selection' solely to kin other than offspring (e.g., nephews and nieces).

Libido: a term used by analysts of all schools to designate a hypothetical form of mental energy. It was originally conceived by Freud as energy derived from the sexual instinct; Jung rejected this as unduly narrow, preferring to conceive libido as general psychic energy that could be expressed in a great variety of forms, of which sexuality was one.

Natural selection: the principle mechanism of evolutionary change, originally proposed by Darwin (1859). The theory holds that of the range of different individuals making up the population of a given species, those individuals possessing certain advantageous characteristics contribute more offspring to the succeeding generation (that is, they have greater reproductive success) than those lacking these characteristics). Provided these advantageous attributes have an inherited basis, they will eventually become established as standard components of the genetic structure of the species (that is, they will be selected by a natural process).

Neurosis: a term dating from the second half of the eighteenth century that originally meant a disease of the nerves; as a result of the work of Charcot and Freud on hysteria towards the end of the nineteenth century, however, neurosis came to be applied precisely to mental disorders that were diseases of the nervous system. Although used less frequently than hitherto, neurosis remains a convenient term for a group of psychiatric disorders that do not involve hallucinations, delusions,or loss of insight.

Numinosity: a term introduced into psychology by Jung, who borrowed it from the German theologian Rudolf Otto. Otto used it to describe what he regarded as the fundamental experience common to all religions—namely, the sense of awe and exaltation generated by the feeling of being in the presence of the Creator.

Object: in psychoanalytic parlance, the term is used to refer to a person, or to part of a person, or to a symbol of one or the other.

Object relations: refers to the social need of a subject to establish and maintain a relationship with an object (usually a mother-figure) and later with other significant people in the subject's life. An object relationship may be with an actual person in outer reality or with the mental representation of that person in the subject's psyche.

Objective psyche: Jung sometimes referred to the collective unconscious as the objective psyche in order to stress its conaturality with all existence: it is as real and as existent as anything in nature. For this reason Jung held that the fundamental natural laws, like the principles of adaptation, homeostasis and growth, apply to the psyche just as surely as to any other biological phenomenon.

Obsessive-compulsive disorder: a fear that things will get out of control and that some catastrophe will ensue; obsessional symptoms and compulsive behaviours arise as quasi-superstitious means to prevent this from happening. Thus patients feel that they 'have got to' think certain thoughts or perform certain acts. Such compulsions can become severely distressing when, as is often the case, they cannot be controlled by voluntary effort.

Oedipus complex: a cluster of largely unconscious ideas and feelings of wishing to possess the parent of the opposite sex and eliminate the parent of the same sex. Freud derived the term from the classical Greek story of Oedipus, who slayed his father, Laius, and married his mother, Jocasta, without realizing that they were his parents. Freud believed the complex to be universal and phylogenetically determined.

Ontogenetic psyche: those psychic attributes that are dependent for their functional development on the personal history of the individual.

Ontogeny: the development of an organism through the course of its life cycle.

Operant conditioning: learning to perform certain acts which initially occur as random or spontaneous movements through rewards (e.g., food) or punishments (e.g., electric shock).

Paradigm: a term given a technical meaning by T. S. Kuhn in his *The Structure of Scientific Revolutions* (1962). Denying that scientific theories are mere products of induction from sensory experience, Kuhn argued that theories give meaning to facts rather than simply arising out of them. A paradigm is the theoretical framework within which all thinking in a given scientific discipline proceeds. A paradigm shift occurs when one theoretical framework is replaced by another.

Persona: the mask worn by an actor in classical times; Jung used the term to describe the 'packaging' with which we present ourselves to the world. The persona is 'a functional complex that comes into existence for reasons of adaptation or personal convenience, but is by no means identical with the individuality' (*CW* 6, para. 801).

Phenotype: whereas *genotype* is the term used to describe the total hereditary information encoded in living organisms, whether or not it is expressed in their life time, *phenotype* represents the actual characteristics—physical, developmental and behavioural—

that are expressed in the course of an individual's life-span.

Phylogenetic psyche: those psychic structures and functions that are characteristic of all members of the human species; synonymous with Jung's term 'collective unconscious'.

Phylogeny: the evolutionary origin and development of a species.

Pleasure principle: Freud conceived the psyche in infancy as being motivated entirely by the desire to experience pleasure and avoid pain; only later, when the ego had developed, was the pleasure principle modified by the reality principle. In Freud's view the pleasure principle operated throughout life as a built-in propensity to keep instinctual tensions at a minimal level.

Projection: the unconscious process by which aspects of the self, or feelings or ideas associated with those aspects, are experienced as if they were located in someone or something external to oneself. Projection commonly functions in association with another ego-defence mechanism, denial, in that one denies the existence in oneself of the beliefs, motives or intentions that one attributes to the person, animal or thing on to whom or which one projects them.

Proximate cause: a term used in evolutionary psychiatry to denote an aetiological factor that operates on and through the constitution and the life experience of the individual.

Psyche: the totality of all mental processes, unconscious as well as conscious, unlike mind, which is conventionally applied to conscious processes only. 'The psyche is not of today,' wrote Jung; 'its ancestry goes back many millions of years. Individual consciousness is only the flower and the fruit of the season, sprung from the perennial rhizome beneath the earth.' (*CW* 5, p. xxiv).

Psychiatrist: a medically qualified practitioner who specializes in the treatment of mental illness. Only a small minority of psychiatrists are also analysts.

Psychoanalyst: an analyst who subscribes to the theories and who practises the therapeutic techniques devised by Sigmund Freud and developed by his followers. Only a minority of psychoanalysts are medically or psychiatrically qualified.

Psychologist: a pure scientist who studies all behaviour, normal and abnormal, human and animal.

Psychopathology: the study of psychiatric disorders and the provision of theories to account for their existence and development in individual patients.

Psychosis: a broad term used to describe those relatively severe psychiatric disorders in which hallucinations and delusions occur in people with relatively poor insight into their condition.

Psychotherapist: a generic term for therapists who use their own minds to treat the minds of others, with or without reference to unconscious processes or using the techniques of any particular school of analysis.

Reality principle: a term used by Freud to designate the environmental constraints imposed on fulfilment of the pleasure principle. Freud believed that the reality principle developed in the course of ontogeny, whereas the pleasure principle was innate and present at birth.

Repression: the ego-defence mechanism by which an unacceptable impulse or idea is rendered unconscious.

Reproductive success: the number of surviving offspring produced by an individual.

Resistance: a term introduced by Freud to account for the unwillingness of his patients to accept his interpretations—an unwillingness he invariably attributed to their reluctance to face the unpleasant nature of their unconscious wishes rather than to the possibility that his interpretations could be wrong.

Schizoid personality: a type of personality structure characterized by a reluctance to enter into close personal relationships, a preference for solitary activities, and displaying a marked degree of emotional detachment.

Self: a term introduced by Jung for the dynamic nucleus of the core of the personality responsible for the process of individuation: the Self incorporates the entire archetypal potential of the unconscious psyche.

Separation anxiety: anxiety experienced at the prospect of becoming separated from a person to whom a bond of attachment has been formed.

Shadow: Jung's term for the aspect of the Self (see) which remains unconscious because it is repressed by the superego, or unactivated because of deficiencies in the life experience of the individual.

Sociobiology: a term introduced by E. O. Wilson for his approach to the study of behaviour; it is based on the assumption that the survival of the gene ultimately determines the form of the behaviour studied.

Superego: a term originally introduced by Freud which has come to designate that inner moral authority or ethical complex which monitors individual behaviour in such a way as to make it acceptable first to the parents and later to society.

Transcendent function: Jung's term for the mutual influence which is exerted between the ego and the Self in the course of personality development and individuation.

Transference: the process whereby a patient transfers onto the person of the analyst feelings, anticipations and notions, which derive from important figures related to in the past. Freud came to view transference as an essential part of the therapeutic process. By remaining detached, and declining to fulfil the patient's anticipations, the analyst seeks to create a novel situation through which it may be possible to interpret to the patient that he or she is behaving as if the analyst were his or her father, mother, grandparent, sibling, etc. This transference relationship is to be distinguished from the analytic relationship (which refers to the total relationship, both conscious and unconscious, between analyst and patient) and the therapeutic alliance (which refers to their collaborative effort to confront and resolve the problems which brought the patient into analysis).

Ultimate cause: a factor contributing to the structure of the human genome over millions of years of selection pressure and determining the biosocial goals to the fulfilment of which human behaviour is directed.

Yielding subroutine: a behavioural program adopted by a contestant losing in a ritual agonistic encounter or tournament. It terminates challenge by signalling submission, and it facilitates voluntary yielding by inducing a mental and behavioural state of 'giving up', 'giving in' and 'giving way'. When prolonged, it may manifest as a depressive state.

BIBLIOGRAPHY

Arlow, J. A. (1982) 'Psychoanalytic Education: A psychoanalytic perspective', *Annual of Psychoanalysis*, 10: 5–20.

Aveline, M., and Shapiro, D. A., eds. (1995). *Research Foundations for Psychotherapy Practice*. John Wiley & Sons, New York.

Baynes, Godwin. (1949). *Mythology of the Soul*. Methuen, London.

Bennet, E. A. (1982). *Meetings with Jung*. Anchor, London.

Belsky, J., Bakermans-Krannenburg, M. J. and van Ijzendoorn, M. H. (2007). 'For Better and For Worse: Differential susceptibility to environmental influences', *Current Directions in Psychological Science*, 16 (6): 300–4.

Bennet, E. A. (1982). *Meetings with Jung*. Anchor, London.

Bergin, Allen E. and Garfield, Sol L., eds. (2004). *Handbook of Psychotherapy and Behavior Change* (fifth edition). John Wiley & Sons, New York.

Bolhuis, J. J., Brown, G. R., Richardson, R. C. and Laland, K. N. (2011). 'Darwin in Mind: New opportunities for evolutionary psychology,' *PLoS Biology* 9 (7): 1–8. <www.polsbiology.org>

Bowlby, John. (1969). *Attachment and Loss, Vol. 1, Attachment*. The Hogarth Press, London; (1971) Penguin Books, New York.

_____. (1973). *Attachment and Loss, Vol. 2, Separation: Anxiety and Anger*. The Hogarth Press, London. (1975) Penguin Books, New York.

_____. (1988). *A Secure Base: Clinical Applications of Attachment Theory*. Routledge, London.

Casement, Ann. (1995). 'A Brief History of Jungian Splits in the United Kingdom', *Journal of Analytical Psychology*, 40 (3): 327–42.

Chance, M. R. A. and Jolly, C. (1970). *Social Groups of Monkeys, Apes and Men*. Jonathan Cape/E. P. Dutton, New York and London.

Conte, H. R., Ratto, R., Clutz, K. and Karasu, T. B. (1995). 'Determinants of Outpatients' Satisfaction With Therapists Relation to Outcome', *Journal of Psychotherapy Practice and Research*, 4 (1): 43–51.

Cooper, Mick. (2008). *Essential Research Findings in Counselling and Psychotherapy*, Sage Publications, London.

Denman, Chess. (1995). 'Questions to Be Answered in the Evaluation of Long-Term Therapy'. In M. Aveline and D. A. Shapiro, eds, *Research Foundations for Psychotherapy Practice*. John Wiley & Sons, New York.

Durlak, J. A. (1979). 'Comparative Effectiveness of Paraprofessional and Professional Helpers', *Psychological Bulletin*, 86 (1): 80–92.

Erickson, Mark. (2000). 'Rethinking Oedipus: The evolution of incest avoidance and psychological kinship'. In *Genes On The Couch: Explorations in Evolutionary Psychotherapy*, ed. Paul Gilbert and Kent Bailey. Psychology Press, Hove, East Sussex.

Eysenck, H. J. (1952). 'The Effects of Psychotherapy: An evaluation', *Journal of Consulting Psychology*, 16: 319–24.

Fordham, Michael. (1944). *The Life of Childhood*. Kegan Paul, London.

_____.(1994). *The Making of an Analyst*. Free Association Books, London.

Freud, Anna. (1946). 'The Psychoanalytic Study of Infantile Feeding Disturbances', *Psycho-Analytic Study of the Child*, 2: 119–32.

Freud, Sigmund. (1953–74). The *Standard Edition of the Complete Psychological Works of Sigmund Freud*, ed. James Strachey, The Hogarth Press and The Institute of Psycho-Analysis. Sources of quotations from *The Standard Edition* are indicated by (*SE*) followed by the volume number followed by the page number from which the quotation is taken (e.g., *SE* 2, p. 44).

_____. (1923). *The Ego and the Id* (Vol. 19).

_____. (1987). 'A Phylogenetic Fantasy: Overview of the transference neuroses', ed. Ilse Grubrich-Simitis; trans. Axel Hoffer and Peter T. Hoffer. Harvard University Press, Cambridge, MA.

_____. *The Freud/Jung Letters*, see McGuire, William, ed.

Frosh, Stephen. (1998). *For and Against Psychoanalysis*. Routledge, London.

Gilbert, Paul. (1998). 'Evolutionary Psychopathology: Why isn't the mind designed better than it is?' Special issue of the *British Journal of Medical Psychology on Evolutionary Psychopath-ology*, 71: 353–73.

_____. (2009). *The Compassionate Mind. A New Approach to the Challenges of Life*. Constable and Robinson, London.

_____. (2010). 'Compassion Focused Therapy', *International Journal of Cognitive Therapy*, Vol. 3: 97–201.

110

Gilbert, Paul and Bailey, Kent (eds). (2000). *Genes On The Couch: Explorations in Evolutionary Psychotherapy*. Psychology Press, Hove, East Sussex.

Glantz, K. and Pearce, J. (1989). *Exiles from Eden: Psychotherapy from an Evolutionary Perspective*. Norton, New York.

Glass, C. R. and Arnkoff, D. B. (2000). 'Consumers' Perspectives on Helpful and Hindering Factors in Mental Health Treatment', *Journal of Clinical Psychology*, 56 (11): 1467–1480.

Grünbaum, Adolf. (1984). *The Foundations of Psychoanalysis: A Philosophical Critique*. University of California Press, Berkeley, CA.

Hattie, J. A., Sharpley, C. F. and Rogers, H. J. (1984). 'Comparative Effectiveness of Professional and Paraprofessional Helpers', *Psychological Bulletin*, 95 (3): 534–41.

Henry, William P., Strupp, Hans H., Schacht, Thomas E. and Gaston, Louise. (1994). 'Psychodynamic Approaches'. In Bergin, Allen E. and Garfield, Sol L., (eds). *Handbook of Psychotherapy and Behavior Change* (fourth edition). John Wiley & Sons, New York.

Hogland, P. (1993). 'Transference Interpretations and Long-term Change After Dynamic Psychotherapy of Brief to Moderate Length', *American Journal of Psychotherapy*, 47 (4): 494–507.

Jung, C. G. The majority of quotations in the text are taken either from *The Collected Works of C. G. Jung* (1953–78) ed. H. Read, M. Fordham and G. Adler, and published in London by Routledge, in New York by Pantheon Books (1953–60) and the Bollingen Foundation (1961–7) and in Princeton, New Jersey by Princeton University Press (1967–78), or from *Memories, Dreams, Reflections* (1963), published in London by Routledge & Kegan Paul and in New York by Random House. The sources of quotations from *The Collected Works* are indicated by the volume number followed by the number of the paragraph from which the quotation is taken, e.g., *CW* 10, para. 441.

_____. (1933). *Modern Man in Search of a Soul*. Kegan Paul, London.

Kantrovitz, J. (1995). 'Outcome Research in Psychoanalysis: Review and reconsiderations'. In T. Shapiro and R. Emde, eds. *Research in Psychoanalysis: Process, Development, Outcome*. International Universities Press, Madison, CT.

Klein, M. (1932). *The Psycho-Analysis of Children*. The Hogarth Press, London.

111

Kohut, H. (1971). *The Analysis of the Self.* International Universities Press, New York.

_____. (1977). *The Restoration of the Self.* International Universities Press, New York.

Kuhn, T. S. (1962). *The Structure of Scientific Revolutions.* University of Chicago Press, Chicago.

Lakoff, R. T. and Coyne, J. C. (1993). *Father Knows Best: The use and abuse of power in Freud's case of "Dora".* Teachers College Press, Macmillan, New York.

McGuire, William, ed. (1974). *The Freud/Jung Letters: The Correspondence Between Sigmund Freud and C. G. Jung,* trans. Ralph Manheim and R. F. C. Hull. Princeton University Press, NJ.

McGuire, William and Hull, R. F. C. (1977). *C. G. Jung Speaking.* Princeton University Press, Princeton, NJ.

Medawar, P. B. 'Review of Irving S. Cooper's *The Victim is Always the Same', New York Review of Books,* 23 January 1975.

Meltzoff, J. and Kornreich, M. (1970). *Research in Psychotherapy.* Atherton Press, New York.

Miller, N. E., Luborsky, L. and Barber, J. P. (eds). (1993). *Psychodynamic Treatment Research: A Handbook for Clinical Practice.* Basic Books, New York.

Miller, W. R., Benefield, R. G. and Tonigan, J. S. (1993). 'Enhancing Motivation for Change in Problem Drinking: A controlled comparison of two therapist styles,' *Journal of Consulting and Clinical Psychology,* 61 (3): 455–61.

Mitchell, Stephen, A. and Black, Margaret J. (1995). *Freud and Beyond: A History of Modern Psychoanalytic Thought.* Basic Books, New York.

Neumann, Erich (1955) *The Great Mother: An Analysis of the Archetype.* Routledge & Kegan Paul, London.

_____. (1973). *The Child: Structure and Dynamics of the Nascent Personality.* Hodder & Stoughton, London.

Noll, Richard. (1994). *The Jung Cult: Origins of a Charismatic Movement.* Princeton University Press, Princeton, NJ.

_____. (1997). *The Aryan Christ: The Secret Life of Carl Jung.* Random House, New York.

Orlinsky, D. E., Ronnestad, M. H. and Willutzki, U. (2004). 'Fifty Years of Psychotherapy Process-Outcome Research: Continuity and change'.

112

In M. J. Lambert (ed.), *Bergin and Garfield's Handbook of Psychotherapy and Behavior Change* (fifth edition). John Wiley & Sons, Chicago. pp. 307–89.

Piper, W. E., Ogrodniczuk, J. S., Joyce, A. S., McCallum, M., Rosie, J. S., O'Kelly, J. G. et al. (1999).'Prediction of Dropping Out in Time-limited, Interpetive Individual Psychotherapy', *Psychotherapy: Theory, Research, Practice, Training*, 36 (2): 114–22.

Price, John. (1967). 'Hypothesis: The dominance hierarchy and the evolution of mental illness', *Lancet*, 2: 243–46.

Roth, A. and Fonagy, Peter. (2005). *What Works For Whom? A Critical Review of Psychotherapy Research*. The Guilford Press, New York.

Samuels, Andrew. (1985). *Jung and the Post-Jungians*. Routledge & Kegan Paul, London.

_____. (2008). 'New Developments in the Post-Jungian Field'. In *The Cambridge Companion to Jung* (second edition). Polly Young-Eisendrath and Terence Dawson (eds). Cambridge University Press, Cambridge.

Shapiro, David A. (1996). 'Foreword to *What Works For Whom? A Critical Review of Psychotherapy Research* by Anthony Roth and Peter Fonagy'. The Guilford Press, New York.

Shapiro, T. and Emde, R. (eds). (1995). *Research in Psychoanalysis: Process, Development, Outcome*. International Universities Press, Madison, CT.

Sloane, R. B., Staples, F. R., Cristol, A. H., Yorkston, N. J. and Whipple, K. (1975). *Short-Term Analytically Oriented Psychotherapy vs. Behavior Therapy*. Harvard University Press, Cambridge, MA.

Stevens, Anthony. (1982). *Archetype: A Natural History of the Self*. Routledge & Kegan Paul, London and William Morrow & Co., New York. New and revised edition: *Archetype Revisited: An Updated Natural History of the Self*. (2002). Brunner-Routledge, London; (2003). Inner City Books, Toronto.

_____. (1993). *The Two-Million-Year-Old Self*. Texas A & M University Press, College Station.

_____. (1996). *Private Myths: Dreams and Dreaming*. Penguin, London.

_____. (1998). *Ariadne's Clue: A Guide to the Symbols of Humankind*, Allen Lane, Penguin, London.

_____. (2000) 'Jungian Analysis and Evolutionary Psychotherapy: An integrative approach'. In Gilbert, Paul, and Bailey, Kent (eds), *Genes On The Couch: Explorations in Evolutionary Psychotherapy*. Psychology Press, Hove, East Sussex.

Stevens, Anthony and Price, John. (1996). *Evolutionary Psychiatry: A New Beginning*. Routledge, London. (2000) second edition.

Tirch, Dennis. (2012). *The Compassionate-Mind Guide to Overcoming Anxiety: Using Compassion-Focused Therapy to Calm Worry, Panic and Fear*. New Harbinger, Oakland, CA.

Waddington, C. H. (1957). *The Strategy of the Genes: A Discussion of Some Aspects of Theoretical Biology*. George Allen & Unwin, London.

Wallerstein, R. (1986). *Forty-two Lives in Treatment*. Guilford, New York.

Webster, Richard. (1997). *Why Freud Was Wrong: Sin, Science and Psychoanalysis*. HarperCollins, London.

Wenegrat, Brant. (1982). *Sociobiology and Mental Disorder*. Addison Wesley, Menlo Park, CA.

Westen, D., Novotny, C. A. and Thompson-Brenner, H. (2004). 'The Empirical Status of Empirically Supported Psychotherapies: Assumptions, findings, and reporting in controlled clinical trials', *Psychological Bulletin*, 130 (4): 631–3.

Winnicott, B. W. (1958). *Through Paediatrics to Psychoanalysis*. The Hogarth Press, London.

_____. (1965). *The Maturational Process and the Facilitating Environment*. International Universities Press, New York.

Ache people, 79
adaptation to loss, 75
Adler, Alfred, 22, 93
Adler, Gerhard, 41, 42
aerophobia, 73
affective disorders, 75-76, 81
affliative behaviour, 78, 80
agonic mode, 78-79
agoraphobia, 73, 87-88
    treatment of, 88
AIDS, 74
algorithms, 84, 90
Alice in Wonderland, 10
altruism, 78, 84-86
amplification, 44, 96
analytical psychology, 21-56.
    See also Jungian analysis
    classical and Fordhamite
    branches of, 44-48
    analytic relationship, 83-
    86. *See also* therapeutic al-
    liance
analytic sessions, frequency
    of, 45, 47, 58, 67
ancestral environment, 27,
    79, 82, 85, 88. *See also* en-
    vironment of evolutionary
    adaptedness (EEA)
anima, 13
animus, 13
'Anna O', 9, 57
anomie, 83
anxiety, 60, 72-74
    'free-floating', 72
archetypal symbolism, 24

*Archetype: A Natural History
    of the Self*, 25, 51
archetypes, 24, 29
    actualization of, 33
    and attachment, 78-80
    biological aspects of, 23,
        51-54
    biosocial goals and, 84, 90
    , examples of, 24
    father, 31-32
    frustration of archetypal
        intent, 51, 82
    as innate psychological
        mechanisms, 29
    mother, 29-32
    parallels with algorithms,
        90
    as products of natural se-
        lection, 23, 71
    rank, 78-80
    as theoretical advance, 29,
        32-33
    two major systems, 78-9
    as unconscious potential,
        24, 32-34, 95-97
Aristotle, 78
Arlow, J. A., 9
Arnkoff, D. B., 68
Association of Jungian
    Analysts (AJA), 43
attachment, 77-78
    'cupboard love' theory of,
        26-27
    kinship and, 86
    rank and psychopathology, 77

attachment, *(cont.)*
  neglect of archetypal basis
    of, 31-32
  theory, 25-28
Auden, W. H., 38
Aveline, Mark, 59

Bailey, Kent, 89
Barnes, F. G. L., 38
Baynes, Godwin, 35-37, 39-41
behaviour therapy, 58
  results compared with psychodynamic therapy, 58
behaviourism, 23, 29, 58
Bergin, Allen E., 59
biological 'fitness', 79
  fundamentalism, 93-94
biosocial goals, 84, 90, 92-93
  and major schools of analysis, 92-93
bipolar disorder, 75
Bolhuis, Jerome, 89
borderline personality, 81
Bowlby, John, 25-28, 44, 86, 93
brain, neuroplasticity
  (changes) in, 90-91
  reptilian, 75
Breuer, Joseph, 9, 57
British Association of Psychotherapists (BAP), 43
British Confederation of Psychotherapists (BCP), 47
British Journal of Medical Psychology, 89
British Psycho-Analytical
  Society, 35

Burlingham, Dorothy, 26

care-giving, 78, 86-7
Casement, Ann, 47
castration complex, 59
Champernowne, Irene, 22, 24-25, 35-36, 39
Chance, Michael, 78
charisma(tic), 57
child analysis, 40-43
Child, The, 29
chimpanzees, 77-78
Christianity, 61
cognitive behaviour therapy, 49, 60, 67
Collected Works of C. G. Jung, The, 36, 39, 31, 42
collective unconscious, 24, 38. *See also* phylogenetic psyche
  as empirical fact, 24
competition, 78-81
  through dominance and attraction, 78
complex, autonomous, 73
  castration, 59
  father, case history, 33-34
  formation of, 31-32, 74
  Oedipus, 59
  parental, 31-32
conditioning, 58
consciousness, 94-99
Conte, H. R., 68
Cooper, Mick, 60, 69
couch, use of, 42, 44-45
countertransference, 46, 63

Darwin, Charles, 22, 84, 91

Darwinism, 23, 49-56, 61, 94
  as unifying perspective, 89
delusions, 72
Denman, Chess, 65-66
depression, adaptive function
  of, 72, 76
  treatment of, 88-89
disorders, of attachment and
  rank, 80-81
  borderline, 81
  spacing, 81
Dodo bird verdict, 10, 60
dominance and submission,
  78-80
Doxiadis, Spyros, 25
dreams, 24, 37, 57, 97
Durlak, J. A., 69

eating disorders, 60, 76
Eitingen, Max, 34-35
empathy, 46, 98
Empedocles, 78
environment of evolutionary
  adaptedness, 27, 74, 82
  contrasted with Western
  society, 82-83
epistemology, 51, 53
'episyemic warrant', 62
Erickson, Mark, 86
Eros instinct, 78
eroticism, 94-95
*Essential Research Findings
  in Counselling and Psy-
  chotherapy,* 60
ethics, 93, 98
ethology, 24, 26-29, 78, 89
evolutionary perspective, 49-
  56

on archetypal theory, 51,
  53
conducive to a new syn-
  thesis, 89-92
dangers of, 93-94
on individuation, 97
on kinship, 83-5
on the life cycle, 51
on psychopathology, 74-
  77
on the Self, 54
on symptoms, 72-77, 96
on the therapeutic alliance,
  83-86
on treatment, 86-9
evolutionary psychiatry, 71-
  86, 96
*Evolutionary Psychiatry: A
  New Beginning,* 53
evolutionary psychology, 90,
  92-93
  renders symptoms mean-
  ingful, 72
  unifying perspective of, 93
evolutionary psychotherapy,
  71-98
*Exiles From Eden: Psycho-
  therapy From An
  Evolutionary Perspective,*
  83
exorcism, 57
explanatory systems, 61-62
extraversion-introversion, 80
Eysenck, Hans, 58

fainting, 73
false self, 71
'family grouping' system, 26

117

fear, 72-73
'fitness', biological, 79
Fonagy, Peter, 60
*For and Against Psychoanal-
ysis*, 50
Fordham, Michael, 37-46
ambivalence about Jung,
39
influenced by Melanie
Klein, 40, 44
personal history, 37-39
schizoid personality, 37-39
stresses transference analysis, 40-2
*Foundations of Psychoanaly-
sis: A Philosophical
Critique*, 62
Frazer, Sir James, 38
free association, 57
Free University of Berlin, 65
Freud, Anna, 26
Freud, Sigmund, 9, 34, 57,
72, 84, 93, 98
derivation of Eros and
Thanatos instincts, 78
Freudianism as explanatory
system, 61-62, 94
Frosh, Stephen, 50, 63-64
frustration of archetypal intent, 51, 82

Garfield, Sol L., 59
Genes on the Couch, 89
genes, strategy of, 84-86, 94-
95
survival of, 84-85, 92
genetic 'fitness', 85
genome, 92

Gilbert, Paul, 87, 89-91
Glanz, K., 83
Glass, C. R., 68
Golden Bough, The, 38
'good enough' parenting, 32
gorgon, 30
Great Mother, The, 29
Grünbaum, Adolf, 62
Guy's Hospital, 24

Haeckel, Ernst, 29
haemophobia, 73
hallucinations, 7
Hamlet, 21
*Handbook of Psychotherapy
and Behavioural Change*,
59
Hannah, Barbara, 39
Hattie, J. A., 69
hedonic mode, 78-79, 90
Henry, William, 68
hermeneutics, 63
Hogenson, George, 55
Hogland, P., 68
homeostasis, 54
Hook, Sidney, 62
Horton Hospital, 36, 38
Hoyle, Frieda, 41
hunter-gatherers, 77
hydroxytryptamine, 90
hypnosis, 57
hysteria, 57

'illness', 96
incest avoidance, 86
inclusive fitness, 84
Independent Group of Ana-
lytical Psychologists

(IGAP) 43, 55
individuation, 34
indoctrination, 50
ingroup–outgroup dichotomy, 79-81, 86
initiation, 51
innate psychological mechanisms, 29, 71, 87
insecurity, 86
insiders and outsiders, 81

Jolly, C., 78
Journal of Analytical Psychology, 41
Jung, C. G., 35, 40, 42, 83, 91, 93, 98
    major contribution to analysis, 55-56
    transpersonal view, 96
Jung and the Post-Jungians, 44
Jungian analysis, 44
    differences between Fordhamite and classical wings, 44-48
    parallels with evolutionary psychotherapy, 95-96

Kali, 30
Kantrovitz, Judy, 64
Kerner, Justinus, 57
Keller, Wolfram, 65
'key worker' system, 26
kin-oriented matrix, 85-86
kin-selection, 84-86
kinship libido, 84
kinship, psychological, 86
Kipling, Rudyard, 73

Kirsch, Hilde, 40
Klein, Melanie, 93
Kohut, Heinz, 46-47, 54
Kornreich, M., 58
Kuhn, Thomas, 69
!Kung Bushmen, 79

Lamarckism, 29
Life of Childhood, The, 41
limbic system, 74
Long Grove Hospital, 38
Lorenz, Konrad, 23
loss, 76

magic, 57
Making of an Analyst, The, 39
mania, 72, 75
manic-depression, 75
Marxism, 61, 94
McGuire, William, 41
meaning, 94-5
    of symptoms, 72-4
meaninglessness of life, 83-84
'medical model', 82-83
Meltzoff, J., 58
Menninger Foundation, 63
Mesmer, Anton, 57
meta-analysis, 60
Metera Babies Centre, 25-28
Miller, N. E., 59
Modern Man in Search of a Soul, 82
monetarism, 61
monotropy, 27-8
mood disorders, 75
Mythology of the Soul, 37, 40

Nagel, Ernest, 62
National Institute for Health and Clinical Excellence (NICE), 48-49
natural selection, 23, 71, 91
Neumann, Erich, 29-31
neurosis, 39, 64, 67, 72, 77, 83
Noll, Richard, 53

object relations theory, neglect of archetypal aspect of transference, 32
obsessive compulsive disorder, 57-58, 72, 76
Oedipal complex, 5
Oldfield, Carolus, 23, 24
operant conditioning, 26, 28
Orlinsky, David, 67
Oxford University, 23-24

paradigm, 69-70
new psychological, 71-98
paranoia, 72
Pavlovian conditioning, 58
Pearce, J., 83
persona, 13
personality disorder, 66-67, 76, 77
phenotypes, 91-92
phobias, 72-75, 87-88
'phobic' anxiety, 73, 87
Phylogenetic Fantasy, A, 72
phylogenetic psyche, 29, 95. See also collective unconscious
Piper, W. E., 68-69
Popper, Karl, 62

pornography, 94
Price, John, 53, 75-76
Private Myths: Dreams and Dreaming, 37
psyche, primacy of, 56
psychiatric disorders, 60, 67, 72
new classification of, 81-82
Psychiatrists, Royal College of, 36
Psychiatry Today, 24
psychoanalysis, as branch of the humanities, 62, 64
as hermeneutic discipline, 63-64
as mode of cultural education, 64, 67
Does it work? 63
Psycho-Analysis of Children, The, 40
psychodynamic therapy, 59
Psychodynamic Treatment Research, 59
psychological kinship, 86
psychological types, 13, 80
psychopathology, 24, 77. See also evolutionary perspective on
basic principles, 79-83
psychosis, 77
psychotherapy, 45. See also evolutionary psychotherapy
as an art, 46, 55
factors common to all forms of, 67-69
use of manuals in, 93

Rangda, 30
rank, 75-76, 78-80
    competition for, 75-81
Read, Herbert, 41
real self, 71
reproductive fitness, 76, 79, 84
reptiles, 75
research, 57-70
    difficulties of long-term, 65-66
    Dodo bird verdict, 18, 60
    hostility of analysts to, 66
    Menninger study, 63-64
    outcome studies, 66
reptilian brain, 75
Research Foundations for Psychoanalysis, 59
Rollin, Henry, 36
Roth, Anthony, 60
Rycroft, Charles, 62-64

sado-masochism, 80
Samuels, Andrew, 44, 48
schisms, between different analytic groups, 42-49
schizoid personality, 37, 80-81
schizophrenia, 81
scientific materialism, 61
sects, therapeutic schools as, 57
secure base, consulting room as, 86
Seeress of Prevorst, 57
Seif, Leonard, 22
Self, the, 41, 44, 54
self-esteem, 77-80, 86, 88

self-sacrifice, 84
shadow, 51
Shapiro, David, 59-60
Sloane, R. B., 59
social matrix, 95
Society of Analytical Psychology (SAP), 41-43
sociobiology, 94
spacing disorder,81
spider(s), 73-74
Stafford-Clark, David, 24
St Augustine, 95
St Bartholomew's Hospital, 38
status, 77, 87. *See also* rank
Stevens, Anthony
    analytic apprenticeship, 36-37
    personal analysis, 22-5
    personal equation of, 21-6, 49-52, 55
    research on infant attachment, 25-28
Strachey, James, 35
stress, 83, 90
Strupp, Hans, 68
submission *vs* dominance, 80
symptoms, as meaningful adaptations, 72-77, 96
Swaby, Molly, 38

tabula rasa, 91
tally argument, 62
territory, competition for, 75-76
thanatos instinct, 78
therapeutic alliance, 37, 46, 83-85
    crucial nature of, 67

therapist's personality, 56, 61, 97-98
threat displays, 78
Tinbergen, Niko, 23
Tirch, Dennis, 89
Tonnies, Ferdinand, 78
trainee analysts, 50
training analysis, 34-37, 44, 54
transference, 33-34, 42, 46, 59, 63, 68. *See also* therapeutic alliance
  archetypal components of, 32-34
  interpretation of, 37, 40-42, 47, 57, 68-69
  kinship and, 85

types, psychological, 13, 80

'Umbrella Group', 44, 47
unconscious potential, 24, 32-34, 95-7
United Kingdom Council for Psychotherapy (UKCP), 47, 58

von der Heydt, Vera, 39

Wallerstein, R., 63
What Works for Whom?, 59
Winnicott, Donald, 32, 54, 93
Wolff, Toni, 22, 35

yielding subroutine, 76

Also by Anthony Stevens in this Series

Title 105. *ARCHETYPE REVISITED:*
An Updated Natural History of the Self

ISBN 1-894574-06-0. Illustrated. Index. 416 pp. 2003. $50

C. G. Jung's concept of the archetypes of the collective unconscious has traditionally been the property of analytical psychology and at times dismissed as "mystical" by scientists. But Jung himself described archetypes as biological entities which must be amenable to empirical study.

In *Archetype: A Natural History of the Self* (1982), Anthony Stevens presented the key to opening up a scientific approach to the archetypes. At last, in a creative leap made possible by the cross-fertilization of several specialist disciplines, psychiatry was integrated with analytical psychology, biology and the social sciences. The result is an immensely enriched science of human behavior.

This revised and greatly expanded edition of Dr. Stevens' groundbreaking book further explores the connections between the archetypes and other fields of study such as ethology and sociobiology, resulting in the new discipline called evolutionary psychotherapy.

Anthony Stevens, M.D., worked in England as a Jungian analyst and psychiatrist for over 30 years. He is the author of several other books, including *On Jung* (1990) and, with John Price, *Evolutionary Psychiatry: A New Beginning* (2000). He now lives on the island of Corfu, Greece.

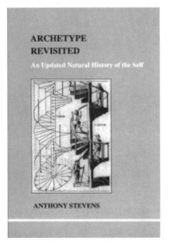

"I recommend Dr. Stevens' book as one of the best introductions to Jung's thought and its practical applications."
—*Dr. Anthony Storr, Times Literary Supplement, England.*

"Dr. Anthony Stevens has made a major contribution to Jungian studies, as well as indicating the common ground between seemingly incompatible disciplines."
—*British Medical Journal.*

See final page for discounts and postage/handling.

Also in this Series, by Daryl Sharp

Please see last page for discounts and postage/handling.

THE SECRET RAVEN
Conflict and Transformation in the Life of Franz Kafka
ISBN 978-0-919123-00-7. (1980) 128 pp. $25

PERSONALITY TYPES: Jung's Model of Typology
ISBN 978-0-919123-30-9. (1987) 128 pp. Diagrams $25

THE SURVIVAL PAPERS: Anatomy of a Midlife Crisis
ISBN 978-0-919123-34-2. (1988) 160 pp. $25

DEAR GLADYS: The Survival Papers, Book 2
ISBN 978-0-919123-36-6. (1989) 144 pp. $25

JUNG LEXICON: A Primer of Terms and Concepts
ISBN 978-0-919123-48-9. (1991) 160 pp. Diagrams $25

GETTING TO KNOW YOU: The Inside Out of Relationship
ISBN 978-0-919123-56-4. (1992) 128 pp. $25

THE BRILLIG TRILOGY:

1. CHICKEN LITTLE: The Inside Story *(A Jungian romance)*
ISBN 978-0-919123-62-5. (1993) 128 pp. $25

2. WHO AM I, REALLY? Personality, Soul and Individuation
ISBN 978-0-919123-68-7. (1995) 144 pp. $25

3. LIVING JUNG: The Good and the Better
ISBN 978-0-919123-73-1. (1996) 128 pp. $25

JUNGIAN PSYCHOLOGY UNPLUGGED: My Life as an Elephant
ISBN 978-0-919123-81-6. (1998) 160 pp. $25

DIGESTING JUNG: Food for the Journey
ISBN 978-0-919123-96-0. (2001) 128 pp. $25

JUNG UNCORKED: Rare Vintages from the Cellar of Analytical Psychology
Four Books. ISBN 978-1-894574-21-1/22-8.. (2008) 128 pp. each. $25 each

THE SLEEPNOT TRILOGY:

1. NOT THE BIG SLEEP: On having fun, seriously *(A Jungian romance)*
ISBN 978-0-894574-13-6. (2005) 128 pp. $25

2. ON STAYING AWAKE: Getting Older and Bolder *(Another Jungian romance)*
ISBN 978-0-894574-16-7. (2006) 144 pp. $25

3. EYES WIDE OPEN: Late Thoughts *(Another Jungian romance)*
ISBN 978-0-894574-18-1.. (2007) 160 pp. $25

Also in this Series, by Edward F. Edinger

See final page for discounts and postage/handling

SCIENCE OF THE SOUL: A Jungian Perspective
ISBN 978-1-894574-03-6. (2002) 128 pp. $25

THE PSYCHE ON STAGE
Individuation Motifs in Shakespeare and Sophocles
ISBN 978-0-919123-94-6. (2001) 96 pp. Illustrated $25

EGO AND SELF: The Old Testament Prophets
ISBN 978-0-919123-91-5. (2000) 160 pp. $25

THE PSYCHE IN ANTIQUITY
Book 1: Early Greek Philosophy
ISBN 978-0-919123-86-1. (1999) 128 pp. $25
Book 2: Gnosticism and Early Christianity
ISBN 978-0-919123-87-8. (1999) 160 pp. $25

THE AION LECTURES: Exploring the Self in Jung's *Aion*
ISBN 978-0-919123-72-4. (1996) 208 pp. 30 illustrations $30

MELVILLE'S MOBY-DICK: An American Nekyia
ISBN 978-0-919123-70-0. (1995) 160 pp. $25

THE MYSTERIUM LECTURES
A Journey Through Jung's *Mysterium Coniunctionis*
ISBN 978-0-919123-66-3. (1995) 352 pp. 90 illustrations $40

THE MYSTERY OF THE CONIUNCTIO
Alchemical Image of Individuation
ISBN 978-0-919123-67-6. (1994) 112 pp. 48 illustrations $25

GOETHE'S FAUST: Notes for a Jungian Commentary
ISBN 978-0-919123-44-1. (1990) 112 pp. $25

THE CHRISTIAN ARCHETYPE A Jungian Commentary on the Life of Christ
ISBN 978-0-919123-27-4. (1987) 144 pp. 34 illustrations $25

THE BIBLE AND THE PSYCHE
Individuation Symbolism in the Old Testament
ISBN 978-0-919123-23-1. (1986) 176 pp. $30

ENCOUNTER WITH THE SELF
A Jungian Commentary on William Blake's *Illustrations of the Book of Job*
ISBN 978-0-919123-21-2. (1986) 80 pp. 22 illustrations $25

THE CREATION OF CONSCIOUSNESS
Jung's Myth for Modern Man
ISBN 978-0-919123-13-7. (1984) 128 pp. 10 illustrations $25

Also in this Series, by Marie-Louise von Franz

AURORA CONSURGENS: On the Problem of Opposites in Alchemy
ISBN 978-0-919123-90-8. (2000) 576pp. **30-page Index** *Sewn* $50
A penetrating commentary on a rare medieval treatise, scattered throughout with insights relevant to the process of individuation in modern men and women.

THE PROBLEM OF THE PUER AETERNUS
ISBN 978-0-919123-88-5. (2000) 288pp. **11 illustrations** *Sewn* $40
The term *puer aeternus* (Latin, eternal youth) is used in Jungian psychology to describe a certain type of man or woman: charming, creative, and ever in pursuit of their dreams. This is the classic study of those who remain adolescent well into adult years.

THE CAT: A Tale of Feminine Redemption
ISBN 978-0-919123-84-7. (1999) 128pp. **8 illustrations** *Sewn* $25
"The Cat" is a Romanian fairy tale about a princess who at the age of seventeen is bewitched—turned into a cat. . One by one von Franz unravels the symbolic threads.

C.G. JUNG: His Myth in Our Time
ISBN 978-0-919123-78-6. (1998) 368pp. **30-page Index** *Sewn* $40
The most authoritative biography of Jung, comprising an historical account of his seminal ideas, including his views on the collective unconscious, archetypes and complexes, typology, creativity, active imagination and individuation.

ARCHETYPAL PATTERNS IN FAIRY TALES
ISBN 978-0-919123-77-9. (1997) 192pp. *Sewn* $30
In-depth studies of six fairy tales—from Spain, Denmark, China, France and Africa, and one from the Grimm Bros.—with references to parallel themes in many others.

REDEMPTION MOTIFS IN FAIRY TALES
ISBN 978-0-919123-01-4. (1980) 128pp. *Sewn* $25
A nonlinear approach to the significance of fairy tales for an understanding of the process of psychological development. Concise explanations of complexes, projection, archetypes and active imagination. A modern classic.

ON DIVINATION AND SYNCHRONICITY
The Psychology of Meaningful Chance
ISBN 978-0-919123-02-1. (1980) 128pp. **15 illustrations** *Sewn* $25
A penetrating study of the psychological aspects of time, number and methods of divining fate such as the I Ching, astrology, Tarot, palmistry, dice, etc. Extends Jung's work on synchronicity, contrasting Western attitudes with those of the East.

ALCHEMY: An Introduction to the Symbolism and the Psychology
ISBN 978-0-919123-04-5. (1980) 288pp. **84 illustrations** *Sewn* $40
Designed as an introduction to Jung's weightier writings on alchemy. Invaluable for interpreting images in modern dreams and for an understanding of relationships. Rich in insights from analytic experience.

Also in this Series, by James Hollis

THE MIDDLE PASSAGE: From Misery to Meaning in Midlife
ISBN 0-919123-60-0. (1993) 128pp. *Sewn* $25
Why do so many go through so much disruption in their middle years? Why then? What does it mean and how can we survive it? Hollis shows how we can pass through midlife consciously, rendering the second half of life all the richer and more meaningful.

UNDER SATURN'S SHADOW: The Wounding and Healing of Men
ISBN 0-919123-64-3. (1994) 144pp. *Sewn* $25
Saturn was the Roman god who ate his children to stop them from usurping his power. Men have been psychologically and spiritually wounded by this legacy. Hollis offers a new perspective on the secrets men carry in their hearts, and how they may be healed.

TRACKING THE GODS: The Place of Myth in Modern Life
ISBN 0-919123-69-4. (1995) 160pp. *Sewn* $25
Whatever our religious background or personal psychology, a greater intimacy with myth provides a vital link with meaning. Here Hollis explains why a connection with our mythic roots is crucial for us as individuals and as responsible citizens.

SWAMPLANDS OF THE SOUL: New Life in Dismal Places
ISBN 0-919123-74-0. (1996) 160pp. *Sewn* $25
Much of our time on earth we are lost in the quicksands of guilt, anxiety, betrayal, grief, doubt, loss, loneliness, despair, anger, obsessions, addictions, depression and the like. Perhaps the goal of life is not happiness but meaning. Hollis illuminates the way.

THE EDEN PROJECT: In Search of the Magical Other
ISBN 0-919123-80-5. (1998) 160pp. *Sewn* $25
A timely and thought-provoking corrective to the fantasies about relationships that permeate Western culture. Here is a challenge to greater personal responsibility—a call for individual growth as opposed to seeking rescue from others.

CREATING A LIFE: Finding Your Individual Path
ISBN 0-919123-93-7. (2001) 160pp. *Sewn* $25
With insight and compassion grounded in the humanist side of analytical psychology, Hollis elucidates the circuitous path of individuation, illustrating how we may come to understand our life choices and relationships by exploring our core complexes.

ON THIS JOURNEY WE CALL OUR LIFE: Living the Questions
ISBN 1-894574-04-4. (2003) 160pp. *Sewn* $25
This book seeks a working partnership with readers. Hollis shares his personal experience only so that we may more deeply understand our own. It is a partnership rich in poetry as well as prose, but most of all it reminds us of the treasures of uncertainty.

Studies in Jungian Psychology
by Jungian Analysts   Quality Paperbacks

Prices and payment in $US (except in Canada, and Visa orders, $Cdn)

Risky Business: Environmental Disasters and the Nature Archetype
Stephen J. Foster (Boulder, CO) ISBN 978-1-894574-33-4. 128 pp. $25

Jung and Yoga: The Psyche-Body Connection
Judith Harris (London, Ontario) ISBN 978-0-919123-95-3. 160 pp. $25

The Gambler: Romancing Lady Luck
Billye B. Currie (Jackson, MS) 978-1-894574-19-8. 128 pp. $25

Conscious Femininity: Interviews with Marion Woodman
Introduction by Marion Woodman (Toronto) ISBN 978-0-919123-59-5. 160 pp. $25

The Sacred Psyche: A Psychological Approach to the Psalms
Edward F. Edinger (Los Angeles) ISBN 978-1-894574-09-9. 160 pp. $25

Eros and Pathos: Shades of Love and Suffering
Aldo Carotenuto (Rome) ISBN 978- 0-919123-39-7. 144 pp. $25

Descent to the Goddess: A Way of Initiation for Women
Sylvia Brinton Perera (New York) ISBN 978-0-919123-05-2. 112 pp. $25

Addiction to Perfection: The Still Unravished Bride
Marion Woodman (Toronto) ISBNj 978-0-919123-11-3. Illustrated. 208 pp. $30/$35hc

The Illness That We Are: A Jungian Critique of Christianity
John P. Dourley (Ottawa) ISBN 978-0-919123-16-8. 128 pp. $25

Coming To Age: The Croning Years and Late-Life Transformation
Jane R. Prétat (Providence) ISBN 978-0-919123-63-2. 144 pp. $25

Jungian Dream Interpretation: A Handbook of Theory and Practice
James A. Hall, M.D. (Dallas) ISBN 978-0-919123-12-0. 128 pp. $25

Phallos: Sacred Image of the Masculine
Eugene Monick (Scranton) ISBN 978-0-919123-26-7. 30 illustrations. 144 pp. $25

The Sacred Prostitute: Eternal Aspect of the Feminine
Nancy Qualls-Corbett (Birmingham) ISBN 978-0-919123-31-1. Illustrated. 176 pp. $30

The Pregnant Virgin: A Process of Psychological Development
Marion Woodman (Toronto) ISBN 978-0-919123-20-5. Illustrated. 208 pp. $30pb/$35hc

Discounts: any 1-9 books, 20%; 10-19, 25%; 20 or more, 40% .

Add Postage/Handling: 1-2 books, $6 surface ($10 air); 3-4 books, $12 surface

($16 air); 5-9 books, $16 surface ($25 air); 10 or more, $16 surface ($30 air)

Visa credit cards accepted. Toll-free: Tel. 1-888-927-0355; Fax 1-888=924-1814.

INNER CITY BOOKS, Box 1271, Station Q, Toronto, ON M4T 2P4, Canada
Tel. (416) 927-0355 / Fax (416) 924-1814 / booksales@innercitybooks.net